/\/WIRED FOR WORSHIP/\/\

small-group study

LifeWay | Small Groups

by Ed Young

Wired for Worship
© 2003 Edwin B. Young
Reprinted March 2011

Published by Serendipity House Publishers
Nashville, Tennessee

In cooperation with Fellowship Resources
Dallas, Texas

ISBN: 978-1-5749-4123-4
Item: 001244598

To purchase additional copies of this resource or other studies:
ORDER ONLINE at www.SerendipityHouse.com;
WRITE Serendipity House, One LifeWay Plaza, Nashville, TN 37234-0175
FAX (615) 251-5933
PHONE (800) 458-2772

1-800-458-2772
www.SerendipityHouse.com

www.fellowshipchurch.com

Printed in the United States of America

CONTENTS

HOW TO USE THIS BOOK

Small Groups are a vital part of how we do ministry at Fellowship Church just as they are in many churches around the world. There are a number of different theories on how small groups should work, and they are all great in different ways. The book you are holding is written with our model in mind. So take a minute to read the following explanation, then feel free to adapt as necessary.

Each of our small groups practices a three-part agenda in every meeting. That agenda includes a social time, a discussion time, and a prayer time. Each of these elements share equal importance, but not necessarily equal time. To help you get the most out of this book we have included an explanation of each of the parts.

The first element of every small group meeting should be a time of socializing. This phase of the meeting should about 30% of your time together. Welcome everyone as they arrive at the host home, make visitors feel welcome by introducing yourself and showing genuine interest in them. Enjoy some snacks, or if your group prefers, a meal together. Then move on with second part of the meeting, the lesson.

The lesson itself may take as much as 50% of your group's meeting time, but remember it is not the most important element. You may want to start this phase of your meeting with a short "icebreaker" to get everyone talking. The questions in the "Start it Up" section of each chapter are what we refer to as "level the playing field" questions that everyone should be able to participate in, regardless of their level of spiritual maturity or Bible knowledge. As your group moves through the "Talk it Up" section in each chapter, remember that it is more important to finish on time than to finish each and every question. It is okay to skip some questions to be sure you allow enough time to take care of the third phase of the small group time: "Lift it Up."

The "Lift it Up" section is a vital part of every small group meeting and should be about 20% of the meeting. During this time you will be able to share with the group what God is doing in your life as well as asking the group to support you in specific prayers. To help focus this time there are one or two questions at the end of each study that will prompt prayers based on the material you have just talked about. There is also a space for you to write down your prayer request(s) so you don't forget them and so you can communicate them clearly when it is your turn. Below that is a place to write down the prayer requests of the people in your group so you can remember and pray for each request throughout the week.

As an additional tool to assist you in your journey of spiritual development there are ten devotionals leading up to chapters two through six. These will help you develop a daily quiet time with God. To get the absolute most from this book I challenge you to take five or ten minutes a day to read and apply these devotionals to your life.

God's best!
ED

Several years ago, I had the opportunity to go to a U2 concert with my brother. We had tickets on the fourth row, and when we sat down, we were close enough to practically touch Bono, the lead singer. The concert was at the Astrodome, in Houston, and was sold out. As we made our way through the thousands of people, I actually bumped into a group of people from my church. When they saw me they all had the same "Is that our pastor at a rock concert?" look on their faces. I wanted to say, "Yes, pastors listen to music, too."

During the concert, I looked around the stadium. I noticed that everyone was standing and singing. Some people were even raising their hands and swaying back and forth. It was amazing to see all these people enjoying the concert together. I looked at my brother and said, "Check this out! Look at what these people are doing; they're worshiping!" These people had worship down. I mean, they were really doing it.

But, at the same time, something else occurred to me. They were worshiping, but they were focusing on the wrong object of worship. These people were giving it up for Bono and the band had great enthusiasm. They had great expressions of worship, but their focus was all messed up.

We all do that, don't we? Whether it is our jobs, our cars, our houses, or even ourselves, we all worship something. But many of us who claim to be Christ-followers don't worship with the enthusiasm, intensity, and regularity the one that we should—Jesus. Too often we think that worship is reserved for one hour on the weekend and that the rest of the week is left for us to focus on ourselves.

We forget that every aspect of our lives is supposed to be about worship—everything we do should be worship to God. This study is designed to help us learn how to do that. Over the next several weeks, we are going to learn how to extend our weekend worship into the rest of the week, through the power of God's Spirit—into everything we do, say, touch, and feel. It is my prayer that, during this study, you will come to understand what worship should be, and that you will clearly see that each of us is wired for worship.

WIRED FOR WORSHIP

SESSION ONE

Acts 17:22-32

You may look at this study, and think to yourself, "Man, why do I need a series on worship? I am a businessperson. I swim with the sharks every day. Worship doesn't really resonate with me. I want something that is more relevant to my life." Take another look. This matter can blow the hinges off your doors and open up a whole new world: the wonderful world of worship.

Start It Up

Every one of us has some interest or activity that we are enthusiastic about, something that energizes and encourages us in the midst of everyday life. Maybe it is something that you do regularly, or perhaps only every now and then.

1. What is one of your "passions"?
   Playing a sport.
   Cooking.
   Gardening.
   Watching the sunrise.
   Playing music.
   Other_____.

Talk It Up

We are beginning a study today on a topic that carries with it as much information and as many interpretations as anything you choose to discuss from the Bible. Worship is huge. It has towering importance because it affects us in this life and the life beyond.

We can't do any kind of study on worship if we don't know what the word means. Most of us probably have only a vague idea of what worship is, so let's start with a definition of sorts. Worship could be defined as having an intense passion or esteem for a person, place, or thing. But for us to understand and get a grasp on this topic, not only do we have to understand what worship is, we also have to understand what worship is not.

Let's consider this first statement. Worship is not manufactured, it is intrinsic. Worship is not something that is fashioned or made up or orchestrated. A lot of people think that worship is just for those religious zealots, those people who bow down in a stained glass cathedral, or who sit in the lotus position humming mantras, or who sway and chant in a religious ecstasy. "Now, that is worship," people think. Wrong. Worship is not a manufactured deal. It is not just reserved for a select group. All of us are worshippers. We are wired for worship. And because of our wiring, we must know what it is and how to do it.

2. In what way would you define the word "worship"? What would you change about the description given above?

Read Acts 17:22-32

Look around you today, and you will see a lot of people worshipping. You will see them being intentionally passionate about a person, place, or thing. They are giving their best thoughts and time to the focus of their worship. You may see people worshipping an automobile, or a dream home; not literally bowing down, but passionate about it, absorbed in it. You will see people worshipping a certain look, or a certain area, or a certain position, or a certain amount of money. There is a lot of worshipping going on. You cannot divorce humanity from worship. We are going to worship something. Paul saw this as he was preaching in Athens. Even though the Greeks did not acknowledge the true God, they could not escape worship. They were worshipping all the time, so much so that the entire city was filled with images, shrines, and altars to various gods. We are created with an intrinsic drive to worship. We have to be passionate about something. If we are not worshipping God, then we will worship something else. We cannot help it.

The sad thing is that too many of us are doing this. We are wasting our worship. If someone were to peruse your organizer, or talk to your friends, associates or neighbors, they could tell just like that what you worship most of the time. You might say, "Oh, I worship God. I worship Jesus Christ. I worship at church." But talk is cheap. Worship is intrinsic; it is an all encompassing activity. We have to remember that worship is played out on a competitive court.

3. What are some things that people waste their worship on?

4. Take a moment to look back on the past week. What got the most attention from you?

When Paul was in the city of Athens, he began to talk about Jesus and the resurrection. The Epicureans, who believed that the gods were unknowable, and the Stoics, who believed we are all gods, were rattled by his words. They invited Paul to the Areopagus to discuss the matter with them. It was here that Paul gave the now famous address that we read a few minutes ago.

Picture him against the backdrop of a city full of objects of worship. The Athenians tried to cover every single base. They had many, many idols, but figured, if they had missed any, they could cover themselves with one dedicated to an unknown god. Paul blew their entire religious system out of the water. Not only does God not dwell in temples, He does not need to be served by humans. More than that, He is the creator, and the one who gives humans life in the first place. Our very being is in Him. We are created to be worshippers. Take a look at verse 27. We have a search engine in our spirit, and we are going to grope and seek and try to find that person, place, or thing to worship. We are trying to get this desire quenched. We move from that thing, to that place, to that person, from that person, to that place, to that thing, and we end up wasting our worship. The only way we can truly find the answer to our worship need is by bowing the knee before God. If you are intensely passionate about anything else instead, you are wasting your worship.

5. God "is not served by human hands, as if he needed anything." Why does he want us to worship him?

6. What does it mean that "in him we live and move and have our being"?

Paul said that God is commanding us to repent of sharing our worship with anything or anyone other than God Himself. Everywhere we turn there are other "gods" competing to get our worship away from the one true God. Satan is very motivated to try and turn our attention in the wrong direction. He wants us to burn up energy and time and wants us to waste our worship, because he knows that when we bow the knee to the true God, when we become intensely passionate about Him, things will start to happen. Things will turn around. Priorities get put in order and life changes take place. Worship is intrinsic, it is all encompassing. It is played out on a competitive court.

7. Why did God overlook ignorance about worship in the past? What has changed so that He is demanding repentance now?

8. What will be the consequences for failing to worship God?

Lift It Up

Let us all declare war over our worship. We need to ruthlessly remove the idols, altars, and shrines that are cluttering up our lives, those things that compete and make us waste our worship. We need to pray a high risk prayer and say, "God, I want to serve You and worship You only." When we do that, we will truly be on-line with God.

9. Is there something we can pray for that threatens to take some of your worship from God?

10. Are there any other areas in your life where you are needing us to pray for you?

Take time to pray for one another.

MY PRAYER REQUESTS

_____

_____

_____

_____

_____

_____

_____

_____

MY GROUP'S PRAYER REQUESTS

_____

_____

_____

_____

_____

_____

_____

_____

_____

_____

_____

_____

_____

_____

_____

_____

_____

BEFORE SESSION TWO

DAY 1: John 14:9b

Anyone who has seen me has seen the Father.

We are made in the image of God. We are referred to in the Bible as the crown of God's creation. No other thing in creation can intentionally be a mirror to reflect our maker like we can. But something bad happened way back in the beginning. Adam and Eve made the call to elevate their will above God's will. They sinned and the mirror was marred. God is holy. Man rebelled against God and messed the deal up. From that day to this, we have been struggling with this marred mirror. At this point, God could have deleted us off the screen. He could have said that He didn't want to mess around with people who have marred mirrors. But God didn't. God loved the world so much that He sent His only son, Jesus Christ, to live a sinless life on this earth. He sent His son to renew the fellowship between God and man, the fellowship that had been broken when Adam and Eve sinned. He sent His son to perfectly reflect for us the Father's brilliance in the Son.

Spend some time today looking at who Jesus is. Choose a chapter from the book of John, read it and meditate on the character of God that is revealed there. Thank God for sending His Son, Jesus, to us.

DAY 2: 2 Corinthians 5:17

Therefore, if anyone is in Christ, he is a new creation; the old has gone, the new has come.

We know that Jesus was arrested; falsely accused for a crime He did not commit. He was tried before Pilate and crucified. He hung on a cross for six hours and right before He breathed His final breath, He said this: "It is finished." He was buried and rose again.

If we come to a defining moment in our lives and make the decision to receive Christ's finished work, then His finished work refinishes our mirrors. He restores our mirrors, remakes them, and refurbishes them for their original purpose. When we are reborn into the family of Christ we are re-silvered, polished, and hung in a new frame. The old is gone, and the new is there to stay. By God's grace, He turns wanderers into worshippers who mirror the majesty of our Maker.

Have you made the decision to turn to Christ and be made new? Praise Him now for His finished work that makes this possible.

DAY 3: Psalm 34:1

I will extol the LORD at all times; his praise will always be on my lips.

Worship is being intensely passionate about mirroring the majesty of our Maker in all that we do and say. Worship should transcend everything that we are about. Press the pause button, and take a look at your life right now. What about your life? What about your worship? Think back over the last week, the time in between church services. Think of every word you uttered. Think about every thought you processed. Think about every image that was before your eyes. Think about those things. What if God took those thoughts, those activities, those interchanges, and framed them, and what if He hung them up for everyone to see? Could God say, "Look, that is worship. This person is mirroring my image in all that is said and done." Could God say that about you?

We have a messed up view of worship. We think worship is confined to a church campus. Worship is a 24/7 deal. Whether you are changing diapers, preaching messages, closing big business deals, throwing touchdown passes, coaching, or teaching, you can do it as an act of worship. Worship must transcend everything we do and everything we say and everything we touch. It is all about mirroring our Maker.

As you go about your work today, look for ways to mix worship with your everyday life. Do you think that the "always" and "at all times" aspect of worship is a part of you? Think of at least one thing you can change to make this a reality.

_____

_____

_____

_____

_____

_____

_____

DAY 4: John 1:8-9

If we claim to be without sin, we deceive ourselves and the truth is not in us. If we confess our sins, He is faithful and just and will forgive us our sins and purify us from all unrighteousness.

Take a good look at yourself. How is your mirror? It is easy enough to look at other people and see that they are full of dirt and spots and wrinkles, but what about you? Not one of us can claim to have a perfect mirror. Could your mirror be cracked because of anger? Is anger holding you back from truly reflecting the majesty of your Maker? Maybe your mirror is foggy because of lust. Is that tripping you up? Maybe your mirror is very ornate, and you struggle with stuff. You don't have things, things have you. Is that keeping you from mirroring the majesty of your Maker? Maybe the mirror is messed up, dirty, because of a character flaw or difficulty. God wants to refinish and refurbish your mirror, and He wants to turn your life into a constant state of worship. He wants worship to define your life. Take a good look at your mirror—but don't be depressed by how ugly it is. He has promised that he will clean us up, faithfully and justly, every time we humble ourselves and confess our sins.

Don't delay. Come before God now, and confess the sins that are marring your mirror. Ask Him to make you a bright reflector of His glory.

DAY 5: Psalm 103:13

As a father has compassion on his children, so the LORD has compassion on those who fear him.

Our worship can move the heart of God. God has feelings, too. For some reason a lot of us think of God as an unflappable, clinical creator just calling the shots.

Think of all of the emotions that you have displayed over the last week. We feel a lot of different emotions in the space of one week. Why? Because we are fashioned in the image of an emotional God. This is a great question to ask those people who believe in evolution: "Explain how we got our feelings." They can't give you a reason. It is because of God.

In Genesis 1 and 2, God calls His creation good. He was delighted with it. When Jesus was baptized, God said that He was pleased with Him. The Bible tells us that God can be angry or sad. David wrote that He has compassion on those who fear Him. It is not a scary fear, it is astonished reverence. God has fatherly compassion on us. Just think about the way a good father feels about His children. He loves them, so His heart is moved when they express their love for Him. God is the ultimate father. He loves us, and our worship can move His heart.

Pause to thank God for your emotions. Write a prayer of praise to God for His fatherly compassion.

DAY 6: Matthew 23:27

Woe to you, teachers of the law and Pharisees, you hypocrites! You are like whitewashed tombs, which look beautiful on the outside but on the inside are full of dead men's bones and everything unclean.

The Pharisees had lots of external stuff. They thought they had worship down pat. They jumped through this hoop and that hoop. Jesus one day looked at them and bottom-lined them. Their worship was all style and no substance at all. They were dead and stinking inside, while they tried to keep the outside nice. The Pharisees were following all the rules. They studied the law. They were serious about the religion thing. But they never brought it to the heart level. There was no spirit. They kept adding to the law and coming up with more and more ways to prove that they were righteous, until they lost sight of the truth. They did not even recognize the Messiah when he came.

Is your life moving the heart of God? Is God delighted when He sees you worshipping Him? Remember that God does not need our worship. He is God. But He wants it because we are made in His image.

Take time right now to ask God to shine His searchlight on your heart. Is He looking at old dead bones, or living worship? Ask God for help in being a true worshipper.

_____
_____
_____
_____
_____
_____
_____
_____
_____
_____

DAY 7: 1 Chronicles 29:12-14

Wealth and honor come from you; you are the ruler of all things. In your hands are strength and power to exalt and give strength to all. Now, our God, we give you thanks, and praise your glorious name. But who am I, and who are my people, that we should be able to give as generously as this? Everything comes from you, and we have given you only what comes from your hand.

Worship changes and alters our perspective. It turns us right side up, up side down. It challenges us. It motivates us. It makes us fearful now and then. Sometimes it is very, very difficult. As David praised God for His glory and power, He said, "Who am I?" This should be what happens to all of us as we look at God and see Him for who He really is. We will look back at ourselves and say, "How can I even look at God?" Yet God sought us and bought us. He made us. He has given us the opportunity to worship Him. When we worship, our perspective will change. We will see that we are only giving back to God what He gave us. We have nothing of our own. The more we worship God, the smaller we become in our own eyes, and the greater God becomes. Worshipping God is sort of like leaving the little cardboard box we live in most of the time and being dropped in the middle of a thousand acre field. When we are in the box, we see nothing but ourselves. Whatever way we look there is an arm, a leg, a knee in the way. We take up all the space, there isn't room for anyone else. When we are in the middle of that big field, the perspective is different. All of a sudden this one little person isn't the biggest thing around. It can be unnerving. We feel insignificant. But the great thing about worship is that when we are standing there feeling small, we are surrounded by love, surrounded by God.

Today, consciously focus on the greatness of God. Let it change your perspective on your life.

DAY 8: Isaiah 6:1-5

In the year that King Uzziah died, I saw the Lord seated on a throne, high and exalted, and the train of his robe filled the temple. Above him were seraphs, each with six wings. With two wings they covered their faces, with two they covered their feet, and with two they were flying. And they were calling to one another: "Holy, holy, holy is the LORD Almighty; the whole earth is full of his glory." At the sound of their voices the doorposts and thresholds shook and the temple was filled with smoke. "Woe to me!" I cried. "I am ruined! For I am a man of unclean lips, and I live among a people of unclean lips, and my eyes have seen the King, the LORD Almighty."

Worship will make us aware of our true position before God. Notice Isaiah's description of the seraphs worshipping. God's angels are not marred by sin as we are, yet they cover their faces in the blaze of God's glory. They realize that they are insignificant compared to God. They know their true position before Him. The same thing happens to us when we see the Lord in worship. Before His glory there is no room for a false view of our own importance or righteousness. Isaiah's response to seeing God was the sudden realization of His sins and of His unworthiness. Ours should be the same. A true worshipper will be a true confessor. The more we worship God, the more aware we become of who He is and how great He is. Before God's holiness, all we can do is beg for mercy. We don't deserve to remain unpunished. But God is merciful and compassionate. Not only does He not destroy us, but He made a way for us to be cleansed. So that we can be in fellowship with Him as His dear children, He provided the ultimate sacrifice for our sins.

Thank and praise God for the salvation He has provided. Take a hard look at your real position as a sinner before God, and worship Him for His mercy.

_/_____

_/_____

_/_____

DAY 9: Isaiah 6:8

Then I heard the voice of the Lord saying, "Whom shall I send? And who will go for us?" And I said, "Here am I. Send me!"

A worshipper cannot just sit still and worship. Worship changes the worshipper. When it is God that you are passionate about, you will find that you have to get up and take action. We see God when we engage in corporate and individual worship, and when we see God, great things will happen. We cannot come into the presence of our holy Lord without being affected. We have to get out and do His business. Real worshippers can't be satisfied to sit around and do nothing. They have to be acting. They long to do His work. Being a true worshipper means a lifestyle change.

How do you think God wants you to take action right now? If you don't have any idea, ask Him about it. Write down the ideas you have and continue to pray about how to carry them out.

_____

_____

_____

_____

_____

_____

_____

_____

_____

_____

_____

DAY 10: Psalm 33:1-3

Sing joyfully to the LORD, you righteous; it is fitting for the upright to praise him. Praise the LORD with the harp; make music to him on the ten-stringed lyre. Sing to him a new song; play skillfully, and shout for joy.

Worship is humbling. It is life-changing. But it is also joyful. Our God is a great God, a holy God, a good and loving God. He is the one who created joy and gladness. He loves to see us praising and rejoicing in Him. Stop and think about who God is. Think about what He has done for you. Isn't that cause for joy?

"Let the sea resound, and everything in it, the world, and all who live in it. Let the rivers clap their hands, let the mountains sing together for joy; let them sing before the LORD..." (Psalm 98:7-9a).

Take this psalm literally. How long has it been since you sang joyfully? How long has it been since you actually shouted for joy? Try it out!

STYLE VS. SUBSTANCE

SESSION TWO

John 4:4-26

We love mirrors. It is hard for us to walk by one without taking at least a quick glance. Some of us do it in a clandestine fashion. Others are overt about it. They just walk up and check themselves out. Mirrors are everywhere: in our homes, in our cars, at the health club, in the boardroom. Even office buildings are constructed with mirrors. We love mirrors, because mirrors reflect an image of who we are. It may sound funny to say it, but this week we are going to see that the subject of worship is all about mirrors.

Start It Up

We can't help being style conscious in this society. Even the most oblivious among us has had the experience of looking at a mirror and saying, "Oh no, I look like I got dressed in the dark!"

1. At what age were you most fashion conscious? How style oriented are you now?

Talk It Up

The most important question a person can ask is, "Why am I here? Am I just taking up space on a planet spinning into nowhere? Am I here just to perpetuate the species, to dream and scheme of collecting stuff, to do deals and to die? Or is there an ultimate purpose out there? Is there a true reason for living? Sadly, millions make their way through this one and only life without ever knowing why they are here or what this life is all about.

To understand the answer to all these questions, we have to go back to the first human beings ever created, Adam and Eve. They never had to ask the "why am I here?" question. They understood why they were in the garden. Adam and Eve saw themselves as mirrors, human beings reflecting the majesty of their Maker. They understood that when they communicated, when they laughed, when they recreated that they were involved in worship. They were mirroring the majesty of their Maker. Everything was going perfectly.

Remember, God always has a passionate purpose behind everything. He created us for worship. He made each of us to be a mirror to reflect His glory. God wants to be able to look at our lives and see Himself reflected back in all we say and do.

Read John 4:4-26

Let's go to another question about worship. Today's title is *Style vs. Substance*. First, let's look at style. How do we worship? OK, we see that we are supposed to be mirrors. We are supposed to mirror the majesty of our maker 24/7. Everything we say and do must be an act of worship. But how do we do it? In thinking about this, take a look at the fashion question. We can talk about style until the cows come home. We have this style and that style, the outfits that let everyone know how rich we are, the outfits that let everyone know what our hobbies are. We have the western look, the suave businessman look, the outdoorsman look, the extreme teen-fashion looks, and so on. But when it comes right down to it, it's just about clothes, just materials to cover our bodies with.

In the same way we can talk about worship styles all day and night. But that's focusing on the outside. Jesus said it is all about substance. We can choose our style, and we can talk about style for weeks. But, remember that worship is a substance deal.

Jesus uses an interchange with a Samaritan woman to teach us about worship in John, chapter 4. He was dealing with a woman who had a bad reputation. Now, no Jew would be seen talking with a Samaritan, let alone a woman with a reputation like this. But Jesus sought out this encounter. He was going to turn her from a wanderer into a worshipper. Why would He choose a Samaritan woman? Why not a religious person, someone who already knew some stuff, to get this great important teaching about worship? Jesus, fully God and fully man, rattles our cages on this one.

2. Discuss the Samaritan woman's statement in verse 19. What is the significance of the argument about worship location? When have you dealt with this kind of argument?

3. Was Jesus' response a change or a clarification of God's original worship requirements?

Jesus summed up worship when He told the woman, "God is spirit and His worshippers must worship in spirit and in truth." This word spirit is the opposite of empty traditionalism, empty denominationalism. Many of us think that if we have gone into a stained glass fortress, eaten a wafer and sipped the wine, or heard hymns or a choir, then we have worshipped. Now, if you have worshipped in spirit and in truth during one of their experiences, then you have truly worshipped. But just because you have come into contact with a little bit of stuff does not mean you have worshipped. Jesus said, "in spirit and truth." There are two interpretations of the word spirit here. Some interpret this word to be the Holy Spirit. Others interpret this word as referring to our emotional makeup, our feelings. Both interpretations will come to the same point.

If we are going to be true worshippers, like the Samaritan woman turned into, we have to worship God in spirit, with our emotions and feelings. We have to be passionate about Him; we have to use the emotions that He has given us to worship Him. However, there is danger when it is just with the spirit. Spirit must be tethered to the truth. You have got to have spirit going on and truth going on. If you worship God in just the spirit, you will get into some wacky stuff. If you are worshipping with just your emotions, without having your feelings tethered to the truth, you will have a church that is out of control and off the charts.

The same thing can happen when a group starts to focus all its attention on the Holy Spirit. You see, the Holy Spirit never calls attention to Himself in the Bible. The Holy Spirit came to be our Counselor. He came to help us understand and apply the truth of Scripture to our lives. When we focus on the Holy Spirit separate from what the Bible says, then we are getting off-line again.

What is he referring to when he says truth? Truth is sound doctrine. Truth is the Bible. We have got to be committed to knowing what the Bible says. We have to be under the authority of God's Word. We have to know and teach and live the full counsel of God. Granola Christians worship in spirit. Conversely, you can have graveyard Christians if you worship just in truth. It is easy for a church to be a graveyard church, the pale and the stale. "Boy, they download a lot of data, but that is about it." It can be just a head game, not a heart game. It ends up being just the facts without the feelings, or the reality of a changed life. You have to merge both, you have to use both the intellect and the emotions to worship. It has to be head and heart, spirit and truth. The Holy Spirit will never motivate, stimulate, or challenge you to do something that the truth does not back up. Sometimes our own self-deceived emotions will though. Sometimes we can get carried away, lost in self deception. That is why we must have the truth of God's Word to check and balance us, to teach and discipline our emotions so that we can turn them to worship in purity of heart.

4. **Apply this to your own life. Do you tend to lean towards intellect or emotions in your worship? What can you do to achieve a better balance?**

5. **How can you tell for sure if you are hearing from the Holy Spirit, especially about issues that don't seem to be clearly defined in Scripture? Share with the group from your experiences in being guided by the Holy Spirit.**

Christ's words in John 4 tell us, "God is spirit and his worshippers must worship in spirit and in truth." We talked earlier about the two possible interpretations of "spirit" in this passage. Well, in John 3, Jesus brings the two together. John 3:6 says "Flesh gives birth to flesh, but the Spirit gives birth to spirit." When we are born again, our spirits are connected to God's Spirit. True worship comes from our spirits made alive and sensitive by the Holy Spirit. God takes the responsibility of worship off our shoulders and places it on the back of the Holy Spirit who energizes our feelings and our emotions. He helps us worship God in spirit and in truth. He helps us to mirror the majesty of our Maker. When you talk about worship, it is not all about you or about me, it is all about God. We should never say, "Oh, I enjoyed that service. That big band was great. Boy, the singers were good.

That one part of the sermon was really funny. I enjoyed it." That is not the response we should have. It should not be whether I enjoyed it or not, but did God enjoy it. Did I sing to Him? Was I engaged? Was I listening? Did I come to worship "worshipping" or to worship God? Is worship a part of my everyday life?

Point of Action

Have you ever heard of a GPS? It stands for Global Positioning System and it is a satellite guidance system that was invented for the military. Today many GPS units are purchased by every day people like you and me as a way to help us get around and not get lost. One cool function of the GPS is that you can use waypoints, pre-determined coordinates, to help you find your way. You go to one waypoint and the GPS tells you how to get to the next one and so on until you have "connected the dots" and arrived at your destination. We have the benefit of worship waypoints that we can follow to help us find our way to authentic worship.

Use these questions as your waypoints to worship: Am I coming to worship service worshipping? Do I worship for my enjoyment or God's? When I sing, is it for Him? Do I listen intently? Do I apply what I learn? Is worship a once a week thing for me, or do I live it 24/7? When you are hitting all these waypoints you are on your way to real worship.

When we truly worship, we move the spotlight off of ourselves and onto God. That is a very difficult thing for people like us to do. The more we worship, the more we understand mirroring the majesty of our maker, the more we understand spirit and truth; the smaller we become and the larger God becomes.

6. Discuss how style might affect substance. Since worship is about God, not about us, how important is it to have a worship style that appeals to us? Should we even bother to think about style?

Lift It Up

Worship: becoming intensely passionate about mirroring the majesty of our Maker in everything we do and everything we say. We have to worship with mind and heart, spirit and truth. We have to be aware of God's Word. We have to be born again, connected to His Spirit. We have to reflect Him. At the end of the day, it is all about mirrors. When we mirror the majesty of our Maker, then and only then, will we know what it means to be on-line, with God.

7. Share with the group about the state of your mirror, about your mind/heart balance in worship. How can you pray for one another as you all seek to become real worshippers?

8. If time allows, share other prayer request with each other.

Take time to pray for one another.

MY PRAYER REQUESTS

_____
_____
_____
_____
_____

MY GROUP'S PRAYER REQUESTS

_____
_____
_____
_____
_____
_____
_____

STYLE VS. SUBSTANCE

BEFORE SESSION THREE

DAY 1: Isaiah 1:18

"Come, let's talk it over," says the Lord. "No matter how deep the stain of your sins, I can take it out and make you as clean as freshly fallen snow."(TLB)

Have you ever had a stain on your clothing that seemed impossible to get out? Sometimes sin seems permanent, doesn't it? We can't forget it, and we can't get away from the negative results of our own wrongness. We begin to think that no one, not even God, could forgive us for this or that sin. We feel like we can never be worthy; we can never be restored. But God has promised us that He can make us as sparkling clean as new fallen snow. Our deep-dyed stain of sin doesn't have to be permanent. Every time we see snow it should point us to worship God because He forgives us.

Praise God that He is the God of forgiveness. Have you confessed your sins to Him, and asked Him to make you clean?

_____
_____
_____
_____
_____
_____
_____
_____
_____
_____

DAY 2: Matthew 6:26

Look at the birds of the air; they do not sow or reap or store away in barns, and yet your heavenly Father feeds them. Are you not much more valuable than they? Who of you by worrying can add a single hour to his life?

Worry, stress, and fear of tomorrow: do you ever find that this is your life? Do you ever think that everything depends on you? This is not God's plan for His children. Instead, God wants us to trust Him. This is not to say that He doesn't expect us to work, it is saying that we have to recognize that ultimately everything is in His hands. We can't make our lives turn out right, all we can do is turn to God and put our trust in Him. Every time we see a bird, it should cause us to worship God. Why? Because God is our caretaker. God is with us. And if He takes care of these little birds, just think how He is going to take care of the needs of each of us, His children. Think about how He will consider and provide for our desires, our wants, the things we don't even know we need. God knows. Let the birds remind you to change your worry into worship.

Every time you see a bird today, consciously thank God for His care for you. Praise Him as God our Provider.

DAY 3: John 15:16

You did not choose me, but I chose you to go and bear fruit—fruit that will last. Then the Father will give you whatever you ask in my name.

Jesus made the first choice; He came to live a sinless life as a human. He chose to die a shameful death, as the ultimate sacrifice for our sins. He rose again, conquering death, and He offers salvation to anyone who would take it. We have the second choice. We either receive, or we don't. And the moment we receive Christ, the moment we apply what Jesus did on Calvary, what happens? Jesus places the person of the Holy Spirit inside of us. And the Holy Spirit's full time job is to help each one of us become a producer of fruit. That's what we are designed for.

Have you made the choice to be a Christ follower? Praise and worship Him today for His gift of salvation. If you have never made the choice to accept His gift, and you want to do it right now, then simply ask Him for it. Be sure to tell your small group about this life-changing decision so they can celebrate with you!

DAY 4: Galatians 5:22-23

But the fruit of the Spirit is love, joy, peace, patience, kindness, goodness, faithfulness, gentleness and self-control. Against such things there is no law.

Just think of your favorite fruit, ripe and delicious, hanging heavy on its branch or vine. You catch a whiff of its wonderful smell, and you reach for the juiciest, most perfect piece. As you take that first luscious bite, stop and think about why God gave us fruit. Of course, it is partly for nutrition. It's also to give us joy—God made the earth "very good." But besides this, God uses fruit as an object lesson for us. A fruit-filled vine or tree is a picture of what we are to be as Christ-followers. God wants us to be fruit producers. Take a good look at the fruit he wants us to produce: each one of the fruits listed in Galatians happens to be a characteristic of Christ. Now these characteristics are not optional. We can't say, "OK, I will produce love by the Spirit. And I like this peace stuff, and I'll take the joy, but let's just forget about the self-control. And don't even mention patience. I am just not the patient type." It is a spirit thing, and the Holy Spirit's job is to point us to Christ. He is our convicter, our counselor and our guide. He is pointing us to Jesus because remember, it is all about Jesus. We have got to glorify and worship Him by producing fruit, by producing His characteristics in our lives. Our Lord said that He would know His followers by the fruit they produce.

What kind of fruit are you producing? Let the next piece of fruit you eat remind you of the spiritual fruit God wants to produce in you.

_____

_____

_____

_____

_____

DAY 5: Psalm 103:15-18

As for man, his days are like grass, he flourishes like a flower of the field; the wind blows over it and it is gone, and its place remembers it no more. But from everlasting to everlasting the LORD's love is with those who fear him, and his righteousness with their children's children—with those who keep his covenant and remember to obey his precepts.

Do you get the point? We are temporal, we are very temporal. We have only a limited time here on this planet, we pass this way only once. Once we are gone, it will only be a short time before everyone forgets that we existed. Just like grass that grows quickly and just as quickly dies or is trampled, we are temporal. Our existence is only a tiny speck of eternity. This could sound very depressing, if it weren't for the rest of these verses. It is true that our time here is brief. But our existence doesn't end with this earthly life. We get to spend eternity with God. He has promised His love "from everlasting to everlasting"—that means forever, that means there can be no time when we are missing God's love. He has promised His love and His righteousness to those who fear him, and God always keeps His promises. Our time is short—use it for His worship and glory. Use it to get ready for eternity with Him.

Think about this verse next time you mow the lawn. Your life is as short-lived as the grass you are cutting, and yet God has poured His love on you "from everlasting to everlasting." Isn't that cause for worship?

_____
_____
_____
_____
_____
_____

DAY 6: Lamentations 3:22-23

Because of the LORD's great love, we are not consumed, for his compassions never fail. They are new every morning; great is your faithfulness. I say to myself, "The LORD is my portion; therefore I will wait for him."

Nothing can quite compare with a sunrise. Even those of us who love to sleep in have dragged ourselves out of bed to witness the beauty of the world early in the morning. The day is new, unspoiled, full of opportunity. And that is like our God. He never gets old, or boring. We can never know all of Him or grow tired of Him. He is a fresh God, a new God. Jeremiah tells us that His compassions—that means His love in action—are new every morning. We can never wear God out. He has a standing appointment He wants to keep with you and me every single day. Too often we call in sick, get busy, or just forget, and we miss our moments with God. There is no way we can live a fresh and vital life if we don't spend time with Him. It shouldn't be a legalistic trip, it has got to be a relationship. We really can know the One we worship. He loves us so much that He wants us to walk and talk with Him.

Watch a sunrise, and worship God. Make a commitment to keep a regular appointment with God every day for a week. These devotionals are a great way to get started!

DAY 7: 1 Thessalonians 4:17-18

After that, we who are still alive and are left will be caught up with them in the clouds to meet the Lord in the air. And so we will be with the Lord forever. Therefore encourage each other with these words.

Let's think about the clouds. We think about clouds a lot. We watch the weather channels, and the announcer talks about this system or that system. We look at the big map, and see where the clouds are, where the storms are, what weather might happen next. When we look at clouds and think about clouds, they should cause us to worship God. Scripture tells us that God has prepared a home for us in heaven. He has prepared for us a place where we will be with Him forever, and Jesus promised us that one day soon, maybe in just a moment, He will return to take us to this home. This is called the Rapture—the word just means "caught up." It's when those of us who are Christ-followers; those of us who are still living will be caught up to heaven one day. We will meet the Lord in the clouds. So the clouds should motivate us to be ready. "Look, he is coming with the clouds, and every eye will see him..." (Rev.1:7).

Are you ready to see Jesus? What do you need to do to get ready?

_____
_____
_____
_____
_____
_____
_____
_____
_____
_____

DAY 8: Genesis 9:12-15

And God said, "This is the sign of the covenant I am making between me and you and every living creature with you, a covenant for all generations to come: I have set my rainbow in the clouds, and it will be the sign of the covenant...between me and you and all living creatures of every kind. Never again will the waters become a flood to destroy all life."

A rainbow, the beautiful blending of sunshine and rain, is one of the most spectacular natural wonders. Part of its fascination lies in the fact that it is not only beautiful, but it is a special sign from God. Whenever we see a rainbow, we know that according to His promise God is remembering His covenant. God made His promise thousands of years ago, and He has not forgotten. Our God is a covenant-keeping God. He still sets His sign in the clouds for us to see, "for all generations," even though most humans have forgotten what it means. But God's faithfulness is not dependent upon human response. He is always faithful; His love never ceases, His mercy never ends. An eye-catching rainbow reminds us of His life-changing promises.

Write a prayer to God, thanking Him for His faithfulness in your life.

DAY 9: Ephesians 5:25b-27

Christ loved the church and gave himself up for her to make her holy, cleansing her by the washing with water through the word, and to present her to himself as a radiant church, without stain or wrinkle or any other blemish, but holy and blameless.

"Washing with water" happens to each of us a dozen times a day. We shower, we wash our hands, we go swimming, we wash our kids, we wash the dishes, we run through the sprinkler, or we step into a puddle. We love water. We can't live without it. We need it not only to keep clean, we need it to stay alive.

Have you ever had to spend a few days with no way to wash? You start to stink. Your teeth get fuzzy, and your hair greasy. Maybe you just don't have time for a little water! You've got a life going. You've got to get moving. Sure, it would be nice to have time to get clean, but you just don't put priority on it. OK, so you would never do that, right? You would not skip your shower and your little date with the toothpaste. Spiritually, we are the same. We need the water of the Word of God to keep clean, we need it to stay alive. Constant application of the Bible in our lives is God's way of washing and bleaching and ironing us, to get us ready to come before the King. What about your cleansing with the water of the word? Do you have time for that? Or do you stink spiritually?

Make a commitment to spend the same amount of time reading the Bible that you spend in the shower every day this week.

_____

_____

_____

_____

_____

DAY 10: Psalm 19:1-3

The heavens declare the glory of God; the skies proclaim the work of his hands. Day after day they pour forth speech; night after night they display knowledge. There is no speech or language where their voice is not heard.

How can we really live a life of worship? We have to learn to be keenly aware of all the ways that God's world points us to Him. We have to learn to involve our whole lives in worship. Make an effort to regularly take a nature walk of worship. All of creation shows His majesty, and His worthiness of worship. No one can escape it. Nature reflects Him, His work, His design. But never forget that it is only that. We should never worship nature. We should never bow down to it. That is pantheism. That is saying that God is confined in nature. No. Nature points us to God. Take joy in His handiwork, praise Him for His goodness, for the beauty He has given us, but never lose sight of God Himself. Make all your life an opportunity to worship God.

Plan a time this week when you can take a walk with God and look for His signs in the world around you. Write down some of the things you discover.

_____

_____

_____

_____

_____

_____

_____

_____

_____

_____

110 HOURS OF WORSHIP

SESSION THREE

Psalm 96: 1-13, Psalm 72:5-7

Not long ago I had an eye-opening experience. Imagine what you would be thinking in this scenario. You take a sandwich into the skating rink, and the owner says, "No food or drink in this rink. You must obey the rules." So, you take your sandwich back outside. As you sit there and eat, you see the owner come out. He goes to his car to get something. You see that he is parked in a handicapped spot, and he is obviously not handicapped. The car sits there for hours and hours. What's going on here? Apparently, rules have to be obeyed inside, but outside it doesn't matter, right?

Start It Up

We are usually quick to spot hypocrisy when it is practiced on us, and we hate it. There is something betraying about a two-faced person, especially when they have a position of responsibility or authority.

1. **When have you had an experience with this kind of hypocritical rule enforcement? How did you respond?**

Talk It Up

We don't like to think so, but often we are just like this. When we come to church and worship, we obey God's rules on the inside; we sing; we clap our hands at the appropriate time. We try to listen and maybe jot down a couple of notes. Then we walk from the inside of God's place to the outside and we end up breaking His laws in spectacular fashion. We check out on the fact that worship happens more on the outside of the church than inside. You may be wondering where in the world the title for this week's study came from. Why 110 hours? Well, in a week there happens to be 168 hours. Let's say you get 8 hours of sleep a night. That leaves you 112 waking hours to do life. If you attend church, let's take 2 hours off from the 112 for corporate worship. That leaves you 110 hours to reflect the majesty of your Maker. We have been learning in this study that worship is being intensely passionate about a person, place or thing. We know that everybody worships something or someone, every single one of us. We have also seen that God demands our worship. He wants it. We are made in His image to give Him worship and glory.

2. What are some things that keep you from worshipping 110 hours every week?

Read Psalm 96:1-13

God knew that we would struggle with this worship thing. He knew that we would have a tough time realizing and living out the implication that everything we do and say and touch should be an act of worship. So here is what our great God did for us. He put in our paths and around our lives many different symbols and things that push us or nudge us towards Him and towards worship. Even the simplest and most common items can turn our thoughts His direction. Most of us have learned a vague "praise the Lord for His beautiful creation," type of worship reminder. This is good. There is no doubt about that. But it can go so much further. The world around us is full of memory triggers that the Lord has provided. Scripture speaks to us over and over again, using metaphors of the things we see every day to help us understand spiritual matters.

3. How are you doing at praising the Lord and proclaiming His salvation "day after day"? What might help you to remember to do this?

4. What reasons are given in this psalm for worship?

We could compare worship to climbing a mountain. The first portion is an easy climb. No problem: just a walk in the park. The trail has been marked; maybe someone has put up signs, or put marks on the boulders to show you which direction to go. After a while though, as you get higher, it becomes more difficult. You find yourself crawling on all fours. Maybe there is a small rockslide. You are all alone, there is nothing there. By this time, you might start to wonder if you will make it. But then you begin to get the hang of it. Sometimes you will hit a plateau. Sometimes you will have to climb down in order to climb up. You may even fall down. But when you get to the top, and turn around and look out, you will be amazed. What a perspective! Everything looks different. What a place to praise God!

Our worship life can be like this mountain climb. We fall down, we plateau now and then, we struggle or get scared by doubt or questions. But we can thank God for allowing us the opportunity to climb. We can thank Him that He has given us little markers along the way, to let us know that we are going in the right direction, showing us that we are becoming true worshippers. So think about this mountain. Think about your progress. Worshipping God in all that we do and say isn't that complex. We just have to learn to think in a new way. We have to learn to see the world around us in terms of worship.

5. Describe a time when you felt like you hit a plateau or took a step back in your life. How did you get past that point?

At first glance, it may seem impossible to actually worship the Lord constantly. Half the time we don't even think about God at all. We get all wrapped up in the here and now, and He is not even part of the picture. We have to change this. We have to become keenly aware of the world around us. We have to learn to see the significant symbols that God has placed in our paths to remind us to worship. Even something as familiar and "unspiritual" as the weather can point us to our God.

Read Psalm 72:5-7

Have you ever imagined what life would be like if the sun and moon were totally fickle? Just picture it—lying awake at night, worrying about whether the sun would come up in the morning; or checking every night as soon as it got dark to see whether or not the moon was there. We are so accustomed to the days and nights remaining the same that we just take them for granted. No matter what is going on in the world, the earth keeps turning, and the sun comes up every morning. The moon continues in its orbit, influencing the tides and waxing full, then slowly waning again. Unless something really weird is going on, like an eclipse, some of us hardly even notice these heavenly bodies. We don't realize that they can be a picture of God's ever enduring presence. Next time you see the sun or moon, think of Psalm 72. God is always there for us. He endures "through all generations." He is the creator of all that endures in this age, and He will endure into eternity to come.

We may not be an agricultural society anymore, but we are all familiar with growing grass. We all like our plush lawns, and some of us really get into it. We get the right varieties of grass, in just the right proportions. We aerate, we fertilize, we declare war on dandelions and moles. Of course, not everyone takes their grass this seriously. Lots of us just mow it and leave it at that. Whatever your attitude about grass, there is one thing for certain: it doesn't matter how much work you put into it, if there is no water it will die. If you see a beautiful emerald green lawn, you know that some serious water has been dumped on it.

Rain is often used in the Bible as a metaphor for God's blessings. In Psalm 72, Solomon is comparing God's presence with us to rain. It is refreshing, cleansing, and brings about growth. We cannot survive without it. When it rains, thank God for His blessings—both the tangible blessing of the actual rain, and also for the symbol it provides of His other blessings. He is like a rain for our souls.

6. Get creative. What other examples from the world around us, can point us toward worship?

Point of Action

The point of this chapter is that when we are awake we should be worshipping. Be proactive in your worship by placing a reminder by your bed so you see it every morning and get up with the right attitude. You may need to strategically place other reminders so that you see them throughout your day. Either way, remember to worship God for who He is, the Creator of the heavens and the earth and every good thing.

Lift It Up

Our world is bursting with reasons and reminders for praising the Lord. Let's make a commitment to look for some of them this week.

7. Where are you now on your "mountain of worship"?
   - On a plateau—I feel like I am going nowhere.
   - On a peak—I have turned around to take in the view.
   - Hunting for a trail marker—I feel a little lost.
   - Sitting on a rock—I am tired and stuck.
   - Scrambling on hands and knees—it is tough going, but I know where the path is.

8. How can this group encourage you and help you?

Take time to pray for one another.

MY PRAYER REQUESTS

_____
_____
_____
_____
_____
_____
_____
_____
_____
_____
_____

MY GROUP'S PRAYER REQUESTS

_____
_____
_____
_____
_____
_____
_____
_____
_____
_____
_____
_____
_____
_____
_____
_____
_____

BEFORE SESSION FOUR

DAY 1: Exodus 20:7

You shall not misuse the name of the LORD your God.

The Bible speaks volumes about the name of God. When God gave Moses the stone tablets with the Ten Commandments written on them, second on the list was the command not to use God's name in a flippant, casual, or profane manner. Some translations say, "do not take the name of the Lord your God in vain." It saddens the heart of God for people to use His name or the name of Christ with disrespect. If someone sacrificed his life to save you, would you trash talk his name? If someone let his only son die in order to save you, would you abuse his name? Would you do that? God is really serious about the honor of His name.

Check over your speech. Are you treating the name of God with proper fear, that is, with astonished reverence for His greatness and holiness? Ask God for forgiveness for the times when you have used His name flippantly.

_____

_____

_____

_____

_____

_____

_____

_____

_____

_____

DAY 2: Psalm 124:8

Our help is in the name of the LORD, the Maker of heaven and earth.

The Bible uses many different names for God. Studying the names of God ushers into our lives a sense of need. We need to worship God specifically concerning His names, because they reflect His character. In whatever situation you find yourself, you can look to God. Among His names you will find one that shows you the aspect of His character or works that will give you hope. Put your trust in Him, praise His name. You will find that focusing on the names of God brings a whole new perspective to your trials.

Make a list from memory of all the names of God that you know. You may think of some that we have not discussed. You may also want to write a list of the attributes of God (omnipotent, merciful, etc.).

DAY 3: Jehovah Jireh: Philippians 4:19

And my God will meet all your needs according to his glorious riches in Christ Jesus.

Are you feeling kind of depleted, feeling that your life is in a kind of free fall? Maybe you should take the name Jehovah Jireh, and worship God because He is your provider. Just think about that: He has promised to meet all your needs! Not just a few, not even most, but all. He will meet our physical needs, and He will meet our emotional needs. He is the only one who can meet our spiritual needs. He provided the perfect Lamb as the final sacrifice, so that we can come close to Him.

Knowing God as the Provider should change our perspective of prayer. Do you ever find yourself praying for something, without any real connection? You pray because you are supposed to, but it would knock your socks off if anybody answered. Why do we do this? It is because we don't really know God. We don't know Him by all His names.

Spend some time thinking of all the different ways that God has provided for you. Write down some of these things, and thank God for each special provision He has made for you.

_____

_____

_____

_____

_____

_____

_____

_____

_____

DAY 4: Jehovah Jireh: John 14:16-18

And I will ask the Father, and he will give you another Counselor to be with you forever—the Spirit of truth. The world cannot accept him, because it neither sees him nor knows him. But you know him, for he lives with you and will be in you. I will not leave you as orphans; I will come to you.

Beyond our salvation, one of the greatest things that God has provided for us is the Holy Spirit. He has not left us alone; He has sent His Spirit to indwell us, to sanctify us, to guide us. Once you are born again, you have the living presence of God in your life.

This translation uses the word "counselor," some others use the word "comforter." Both words capture only a part of the function of the Holy Spirit. Some people like to think of Him as "the one who comes alongside," highlighting the role the Holy Spirit has in teaching, guiding, correcting, supporting and comforting us. When we accept the gift of salvation, when we ask God to apply the blood of Christ's sacrifice to our lives, the Holy Spirit comes in and begins to change us from the inside out.

Write down some of the ways in which you have seen the Holy Spirit at work in your life lately. Praise God for the way He is changing you into a mirror for His glory.

DAY 5: Jehovah Nissi: John 16:33

I have told you these things, so that in me you may have peace. In this world you will have trouble. But take heart! I have overcome the world.

Are you finding yourself in the midst of a battle? Or do you see one on the horizon? This is the time to remember His name, Jehovah Nissi. The Lord is your banner, your victory standard. When you are struggling against sin, you have the assurance that God is on your side, and that therefore you can win. When you feel that the evil in the world is overpowering you, and you can't find where the good is, you have the assurance that God is the ultimate victor.

Get the picture of what was going on when Jesus spoke these words to his disciples. He knew that in a very short time He would be arrested, subjected to a mockery of a trial, brutally beaten and unjustly put to a shameful death. His disciples would have to see all this happen. They would have to watch their Master, their best friend swept along in a tide of unchecked evil. And Jesus, knowing what would happen, offered them peace. Peace? "Trouble is coming," He said, "but don't be scared. I've already won!" When we are in the midst of trouble, we can't see ahead and understand God's plan any more than the disciples could comprehend the glorious results of those tragic last days. But when those times come, we can remember and cling to God who has already won the victory.

Write down 1 Corinthians 15:57. Memorize it and meditate upon it.

DAY 6: Jehovah Shalom: John 14:27

Peace I leave with you; my peace I give you. I do not give to you as the world gives. Do not let your hearts be troubled and do not be afraid.

When you think about victory, what comes to mind? Maybe you think of rejoicing first. When a great victory has been won, people dance in the streets. They give parties, they parade around and wave flags and blow trumpets. But after the first rush of relief and joy, the aim and result of victory is peace. God is the God of peace, and peace is His gift to us. Knowing that His ultimate victory is assured, we can rest in His peace now, as though it was all already over.

The peace of God isn't something that can be understood easily. On the face of it, it often just does not make sense. When Jesus told His disciples that He was leaving His peace with them, He knew that they were on the verge of some heart-wrenching trouble. The kind of peace He offers is not peace in the bucolic sense, where it is peaceful because nothing ever happens. He is talking about a peace inside, a peace of the soul which enables the believer to undergo all kinds of trials and persecutions without delaminating. This is the kind of peace that allowed Paul and Silas to worship and sing in prison, rather than groaning and moaning or frizzling out with fear. It is a powerful peace, and it is available to us. So, next time you are afraid, turn to Jehovah Shalom and let His peace fill your heart.

Write Philippians 4:7 out on a card and stick it up in some place where you will see it frequently.

_____
_____
_____
_____

DAY 7: Jehovah Meqaddesh: Hebrews 10:10b

...we have been made holy through the sacrifice of the body of Jesus Christ once for all.

Maybe you are dealing with sin. Maybe you are locked on the rearview mirror of your life; you can't get your eyes off what you did in the past and move on. This is the time to remember Jehovah Meqaddesh, the Lord who makes you holy. You know, God requires that we be holy. Not just kind of good, but perfect even as He is perfect. And you know what else? We can't do it. We can't even be kind of good all the time. Even on our best days, we blow something. We say something mean. We leave something undone. We fail to mirror the majesty of our Maker. We complain instead of worshipping. When we start to think about what we are really like, it gets pretty depressing. How can we ever make it? Well, the good news is this: we can't make it, but God is the God who sanctifies, and He does it for us. Through Christ's death, we can be purified. We can be washed clean, made into new creatures. This doesn't mean that we don't still mess up. We all will. But we can know that if we turn to God and repent, He will cleanse us. Over and over again. Because Christ's death paid for it all. And as we turn to him for cleansing, we will find that He is working sanctification in us. He cleans up more and more areas of our lives so that we can reflect His image.

In what areas do you need to come to God with confession, and ask for cleansing?

_____
_____
_____
_____
_____
_____

DAY 8: Jehovah Ropi: John 10:11, 14

I am the good shepherd. The good shepherd lays down his life for the sheep. I am the good shepherd; I know my sheep and my sheep know me.

This may come as news to some of you, but sheep are actually really dumb. If one sheep panics, all the rest panic too. If one sheep finds a way to get out of the pasture, all the rest will too—even if the pasture is full of lush grass, and there are only weeds on the outside. A sheep will get its head caught in the same hole in the fence again, and again, and again. Sheep are vulnerable to wild animals, they have no way to defend themselves. Sheep need to be constantly looked after. Now, while it is true that sheep are pretty dumb, they are smart enough to recognize their protector. A flock of sheep will learn the sound of their shepherd's voice, and they will come when the shepherd calls. They associate that voice with comfort, with food and salt and the hands that dress their wounds and help them with their lambs.

It should be pretty humbling to realize that we are quite a lot like sheep. We need someone to protect us and keep us from going astray. We need someone to feed us and dress our wounds, to help us and comfort us. We need a shepherd. The great thing is realizing that we have the ultimate shepherd. We have Jehovah Rophi, the Lord our Shepherd. Our shepherd does not only lead and feed us. Jesus laid down His life for us, He went all the way to keep us safe.

How does it make you feel to think of God as your shepherd? Do you recognize His voice? How can you become more familiar with its sound?

_____

_____

_____

_____

DAY 9: Jehovah Raphah: 1 Peter 2:24

He himself bore our sins in his body on the tree, so that we might die to sins and live for righteousness; by his wounds you have been healed.

If there is one thing that everyone has heard about Jesus' life, it is his healing ministry. Even those who don't believe it really happened are irresistibly attracted to the idea of a man who could actually go around relieving the suffering of ordinary people. Throughout the gospels, the theme recurs again and again: "He healed them all," "and Jesus healed him," "Jesus healed many who had various diseases," "immediately her bleeding stopped," and many more. We are all familiar with bodily illness, and often we long for Jesus to heal us, as he did for those multitudes two thousand years ago. Sometimes He still does miraculous healings, for He is the Great Physician, the Lord our Healer. But His healing goes far deeper that merely dealing with our physical infirmities. Every one of us is sick in our souls, sick with sin. David cried out to the Lord saying, "O LORD, have mercy on me; heal me, for I have sinned against you." (Psalm 41:4). Later on, God spoke through the prophet Isaiah, saying of the humans He had created, "I have seen his ways, but I will heal him; I will guide him and restore comfort to him." (Isaiah 57:18). Through Christ's death on the cross, our sin-sick souls can be healed and restored. His wounds are our salvation.

Do you need healing in your life right now, either physical or spiritual? Do you know someone who does? List these needs now, and pray for God's healing. Be sure to record the answers to these prayers.

Harold Simmons

Bob Young

Shelby

Linda

DAY 10: Revelation 3:5

He who overcomes will, like them, be dressed in white. I will never blot out his name from the book of life, but will acknowledge his name before my Father and his angels.

Philippians 4:3b

...and the rest of my fellow workers, whose names are in the book of life.

All of us know the name of God, and obviously God knows our names, but has your name been registered in the Book of Life? The moment that we make the decision to receive the redemptive work of Christ on the cross, when we acknowledge that Jesus is the only way we can get to God, then our names will be recorded in the Lamb's Book of Life. Jesus was called the Lamb of God. All the Old Testament sacrifices point to the ultimate lamb, the final sacrifice of Christ. If you have not responded to Christ, if you have not come before God and said, "I confess that I am a sinner. I want the blood of Christ's sacrifice to apply to me. I want to be a Christ follower," then your name is not in His Book of Life. It doesn't matter if you have grown up in church, if you cut your teeth on the back pew of a house of God, if you have been baptized and confirmed. It is all immaterial unless your name is recorded in the Lamb's Book of Life. Is your name there? When you face God after your death, will He find you in His book?

Are you relying on your upbringing to make you right with God? You may believe in Him, but have you actually made the step to become a child of God? If not, you can make that decision today. Be sure and share this decision with your small group so they can celebrate with you!

_____

_____

THE ULTIMATE
INTRODUCTION

SESSION FOUR

Exodus 3:13-15

Over the past few weeks we have been delving into the wonderful world of worship. In the last chapter, we talked about the fact that God has placed significant symbols in our paths to point us to worship. Today we are going to talk about the names of God. Just by understanding, articulating, and defining the names of God, we should be drawn to worship.

Start It Up

Life is full of awkward moments. One of the worst is the "name loss" moment. You are standing at a party talking to some good friends. Suddenly out of the corner of your eye you see someone approaching. As you lock eyes with them, you know you should remember that person's name, but you can't come up with it. As this unknown friend comes closer, your good friends give you this look that says, "Aren't you going to introduce me?" In a nanosecond you have to make a choice. Number one, you can look at your approaching friend and say, "I'm sorry. I have forgotten your name and I am also an idiot." Or, number two, you can just kick back for a second and pray that your friends will somehow introduce themselves to each other, and no one will know that you forgot.

1. Recall a time when you forgot someone's name, or failed to make an important introduction. What happened?

Talk It Up

Names are so important to us. Knowing the names of your acquaintances lets them know that you think about them, that they are important to you. No one ever forgets the name of a person close to them. If you came up to someone and said, "This is my best friend, but I don't know his name. I don't really spend that much time with him," everyone would think you had some major social maladjustment problems. So, what if you were in a conversation with a group of friends at a party, and God walked up. Could you introduce him? Do you really know who he is, his true nature and character, his essence? Sadly, most of us can say the name of God, but we don't really know who he is and what he is all about. When you say the name of God, what comes into your mind? A detached bearded deity in a long, white flowing robe, who is busy tweaking the dials of the universe? A denominational God, who is confined and defined by a particular church or creed? A benevolent God, always smiling no matter what we do? What do you think of first? Do you really know him?

Think of a well-known name, perhaps an actor. You know this actor by his name and profession. But his wife knows him by another name. She knows what kind of husband he is. His kids know him as dad. His mom knows him as her son. His agent knows him as a client. We can know the name of this person, but to really know his true essence we would have to understand and see him in different roles. We would have to know him by different names.

Psalm 113:2 says, "Let the name of the Lord be praised." The name of the Lord should be worshipped. However, we can't praise His name if we don't really know His name.

Read Exodus 3:13-15

This name of God, "I AM" is the most commonly used name of God in the Bible. For those who are into statistics, it is used 6,800 times throughout the pages of Scripture. In some translations it is written "Jehovah." Many translations represent this name of God with the word LORD written all in capital letters. The word is made up of four Hebrew letters, represented in English letters as YHWH. This name was so holy to the Israelites that they would not even pronounce it. Far from using it flippantly, they were concerned that even in writing the letters the name should be shown respect.

2. What does the name "I AM" tell us about God? What does this mean for me?

Read Genesis 1:1

This is the word Elohim. This name is commonly used in the Old Testament for God. It is the name used in the creation story. Elohim, the creator. It is simply translated "God" in our English Bibles. Interestingly, this name is in the plural form.

3. Discuss the implications of the plurality of this name "Elohim." For extra insight read John 1:1,14.

Read Psalm 91:1

Each of the names of God portrays a different aspect of his nature and character. He is "I AM," defined only by Himself. He is Elohim, God in three persons, the creator of the universe and more wonderful than any of it. He is El Shaddai, the Almighty, our safe place, our trustworthy protector and provider. He also has another name, and sometimes this one is a little harder to say: Lord. His name Adhonai, Lord, has two big implications: first, God's dominion, His lordship. The second implication is our submission and our stewardship. If we got this one right we would be different people, we wouldn't skim the surface any more.

Read Psalm 16:2

4. When have you experienced God as El Shaddai? When have you experienced him as Adhonai?

5. How should knowing these four different names of God affect the way we respond to him?

Besides these four main names, God also has several names connected to the name Jehovah. Some call them the compound names of God. They could also be called the redemptive names of God, because each name highlights a part of His redemptive character. Each name has a story to go with it, detailing how God revealed this part of Himself to humankind.

Choose one of the following names of God to discuss.

JEHOVAH JIREH
Read Genesis 22:13-14

The setting: Mt. Moriah. The players: Abraham, his only son Isaac, and God. God asks Abraham to do something strange. He asks Abraham to sacrifice his only son as a burnt offering. Abraham says, "Yes God, I will do it." Scripture records that Abraham saddled up a donkey with everything he needed for the sacrifice. He took Isaac and a couple of servants. They began to walk toward Mt. Moriah. They spotted the mountain in the distance. Genesis 22:5, "He said to his servants, stay here with the donkey while I and the boy go over there, we will worship and we will come back to you." Can you imagine what was going on in Abraham's mind? Can you imagine the conversation he had with his only son as he was walking up Mt Moriah knowing that he was going to take his son's life? When Isaac questioned his father about the animal to be sacrificed, his father only answered that God would provide.

Abraham tied his son to the altar, and as he was unstrapping his knife, an angel of God said, "Abraham, don't touch your son. Now I know you are a true man of God, you would even give up your son. Take him off the altar. Then he showed Abraham a ram caught in the thicket. Abraham captured the ram and sacrificed it. And on Mt. Moriah Abraham named the spot "Jehovah Jireh", "the LORD is my Provider." On this same mountain, many years later, Solomon built the temple. It is where all of the temple sacrifices took place. Later in the same place, God put His own son on the cross. There wasn't a voice from heaven saying, "stop." There wasn't a ram in the thicket. Christ did it because of His unfathomable love for you and me. He became our ultimate sacrifice.

In His redemptive work on the cross—the most amazing act of grace that will ever be known to us—Jesus has provided a way for us to know God. The word "provide" comes from two Latin words, which could roughly be translated "first" or "ahead" and "to see." God knows the future. He has looked ahead. There is not a need or a question that we can bring to God that He is not ready for, that He is not equipped to deal with. He has already processed the information. He is Jehovah Jireh, our God who provides.

6. **How has Jehovah Jireh provided for you this week? How can you recognize Him for His provision?**

JEHOVAH NISSI
Read Exodus 17:15-16

The Amalekites were some evil people. Strangely enough, they lived in the region of the Dead Sea. That could make you mean just living there. The Amalekites killed people for sport, tortured people, and dominated people. The stumbling Israelites showed up in their region, and the Amalekites were licking their chops believing they could easily take out the Hebrew hicks. Moses was on a mountain overlooking the whole scene. He talked to Joshua and told him to take some men and go rumble with the Amalekites. He promised to lift his hands and pray and seek God.

Joshua took on the Amalekites and Moses lifted his rod and prayed. The Israelites began to win the battle. However, when Moses' hands became tired, the Amalekites began to win. Moses had two friends with him, Aaron and Hur. When Moses' arms began to get heavy, they helped hold them up. Miraculously the Israelites defeated the Amalekites. So what did Moses do? Did he just high five Aaron and Hur and say, "Yeah, man, we did it!"? No, he cruised down the mountain and built a memorial, and he named it Jehovah Nissi: "the LORD is my Banner." Jehovah is our victory flag, the standard we march under. Moses wanted to mark this spot to indicate that this was the place where God was a God of victory.

7. Most of us see banners and flags everyday, and we recognize what they represent—from our country to our favorite sports team. How can we better acknowledge Jehovah Nissi in the battles we fight?

JEHOVAH MEQADDESH
Read Leviticus 20:7-8

At the count of three, let's breathe a huge sigh of relief. Personalize this text to yourself. God is saying to each of us, "You shall keep my statutes. I will sanctify you. You can't sanctify yourself. You can't make yourself holy. I will do it!"

Jehovah Meqaddesh is "the LORD who makes me holy." The Lord cleanses. The word sanctification simply means to be set apart to be used by God. It is used 700 times just in the Old Testament. God is holy. He wants us to be holy, sanctified, set apart for Him. On our own, we cannot make it. We cannot be holy. That is why we can heave a sigh of relief when we learn this name of God. He will do the sanctifying work. He will make us become mirrors of His majesty.

Remember in the Old Testament how God used the temple for His dwelling place? It was the place where He manifested himself in a special way, where He let His Presence be felt and known. Well, in the New Testament, He changed this pattern. I Corinthians 3:16 says, "Don't you know that you yourselves are God's temple and that God's Spirit lives in you?" The moment in time when we make the choice to make a temple out of our life, and allow Christ to come in, He places the Holy Spirit there. The Holy Spirit works from the inside out to make us holy, pure and clean.

8. How does knowing that you are God's temple affect how you live?

9. How have you seen the Holy Spirit working in your life? Encourage one another by sharing one way God has changed you.

JEHOVAH ROPHI
Read Psalm 23:1-6

Jehovah Rophi, the LORD is my shepherd. He is my director, my leader. As you peruse the rest of the Bible, you will see time and time again that we are compared to sheep. Now if you know anything about sheep, you will know that this is not a very flattering comparison. But it does provide us with an incredible picture of who God is. We are like sheep, in need of a shepherd. We can't make it on our own, we have neither the sense nor the power to protect and feed ourselves. We don't know where to go or what to do. We need someone to take care of us. And we don't deserve it.

Here is the problem we have with the Christian life. We think about being specific with our sins and confessing them and that is good. But we forget to ask God to forgive us for being dumb humans. We are unworthy before him. We are Dead Sea people. Nothing is living inside without Him. It is like the prophet Isaiah when he saw God. "I am unclean God, on my best day, I don't measure up." Is God your shepherd, your guide?

10. What dangers might a sheep without a shepherd face? How do those compare to the dangers we face without God guiding and protecting us?

Lift It Up

We have just scratched the surface in this study, but even the short time we have spent in looking at God's names should bring into your life a true sense of awe. You cannot study the names of God without being awed. Read the book of Acts. It said people in the early church were filled with a sense of awe. That is a sense of astonishment. We must be astonished by the nature and character of God, that He would love and reveal Himself specifically to people like us.

We have been talking about the names of God. Be candid. Speaking of names, name the name of the one who gives you more problems in worship than anyone or anything. Yes that is right. It is yourself.

11. **Which of the names of God that we have looked at really speaks to a situation you are in now? How can we pray for that situation?**

Point of Action

You have learned several of God's names in this discussion and there are many more that have not been mentioned. Choose one that interests you and write it down. Now write down what it means. Begin recording everything that this name and its meaning makes you think of. How does it help you understand Him better? What stories from your own life come to mind?

Take time to pray for one another.

MY PRAYER REQUESTS

_____
_____
_____
_____
_____

MY GROUP'S PRAYER REQUESTS

_____
_____
_____
_____
_____
_____
_____
_____

THE ULTIMATE
INTRODUCTION

BEFORE SESSION FIVE

DAY 1: Ephesians 6:18-19

Pray in the Spirit on all occasions with all kinds of prayers and requests. With this in mind, be alert and always keep on praying for all the saints.

A lot of us have some misconceptions about prayer. We think that we have to be in a certain place, or a certain position. We imagine that we have to use flowery language, and well-turned phrases. We think that we can't possibly pray all the time, as the Scripture tells us to. Prayer isn't hard. It is simply talking to God. We don't have to be kneeling down, though it is good to do that sometimes. We don't have to be eloquent. That is part of what praying in the Spirit means. God knows what we need, and when we don't know what to say, the Spirit will intercede for us.

You can talk to God anywhere, at anytime. Ask Him for healing, for wisdom, for insight into your affairs. Confess your sins, praise Him, pray for others, and pray for your loved ones. Pray for the unbelievers you know, that they will be drawn to Him. Pray for your brothers and sisters in Christ, that they would grow and be brought on to the next level of faith. And pray for your church leaders. Ask God to give them wisdom, ask for His protection on their hearts and lives and families. Your prayers will make a difference.

Find something that you can use as a prayer reminder (a note to yourself, a small cross, or some other symbol). Put it in your car or other strategic places and use it to remind you to talk to God as you go about your ordinary day.

_____
_____
_____

DAY 2: James 3:1

Not many of you should presume to be teachers, my brothers, because you know that we who teach will be judged more strictly.

You know, teaching is serious business. We have talked about being prepared before you come when you are part of the congregation. What about when you are a part of the leadership? What about when you are going to be ministering to others? That is the time when we need to take preparation even more seriously.

Say you invited some friends over to your place on Friday night. You tell them you will see them around seven. At seven on Friday you hear that knock on the door. Would you greet your invited guests, unshaven and in an old T-shirt? Would the den be an absolute mess with clothes everywhere?

Instead, you would think through the evening. You would put on something that looks halfway decent. You would clean the house and have some music playing. You would prepare food in a creative way. You might even light some candles. Is that being hypocritical? Is that not being real? No, that is thinking about the guests, and their needs. That is precisely what we must do when we are preparing to teach and minister. We must be ready. The stakes are high, and sometimes you may have only a few minutes, an hour or so, to touch a person's life.

In the way God has set up His church, every believer ends up being a teacher to someone at some point. Upon whom might you have this kind of teaching influence? What do you need to do to prepare a spiritual "meal" for this person?

_____
_____
_____

DAY 3: Psalm 63:1

Oh God, you are my God, earnestly I seek you; my soul thirsts for you, my body longs for you, in a dry and weary land where there is no water.

Our relationship with God, the desire to worship Him, should be the driving force in our lives. It has got to be the priority. Have you ever been really thirsty? At first, your throat and tongue may feel just a little dry. You think, "I'd like a nice cool, tall glass of water." If this goes on, pretty soon you will not just be thirsty, you will feel sick. You will be suffering from dehydration. You may have a headache or feel nauseated. After a while, all you can think about is water. Nothing, nothing in the world sounds even remotely interesting except water. You have got to have it to survive.

That is the way our souls should be about God. He is what keeps us going. If we neglect our relationship with Him, we will dry up spiritually. We will become sick. Our spirits have to be continually connecting with God in the same way our bodies continually need water. It isn't just a one time fix. We have to keep coming to God. You wouldn't say, "I just don't have time to get a drink. It won't matter if I dehydrate a little. I've got stuff to do." How are you treating your relationship with God? Is it a priority?

Make a list of what you think your priorities should be. Make a list of what they really end up being. What can you do to help make your second list match the first one better?

_____

_____

_____

_____

_____

DAY 4: 1 Samuel 16:7

... The LORD does not look at the things man looks at. Man looks at the outward appearance, but the LORD looks at the heart.

We humans have the strangest fixation with fashion. When it comes right down to it, it is just about fabric to cover our bodies, but we add a whole lot more to it than that. Sometimes we make church into a fashion parade. We say, "I cannot wait until Sunday, I just want to put on my new outfit, and let everybody see how nicely I can dress." Sometimes it works the other way. We say, "I don't have anything nice. I can't go to church. I will look out of place." This is all wrong. We have things turned upside down. God says that He is not looking at the outside, like we do. He is interested in what we are like inside. Are you coming to church to meet with God, or to be seen by the rest of the congregation? Is your heart clean, are you in fellowship with God, are you loving Him? Or are you covering up a heart that is filthy with sin, a heart that has grown cool towards Him, a heart that is indifferent or tired of trying? Instead of looking in your closet this week, look into your heart. Have you confessed your sins? Are you harboring bitterness, or anger or unforgiveness? Are you eager to obey, or are you holding on to something you're afraid He'll ask you to give up? Put your heart in order first. Your outside appearance is not the important part.

Ask God to show you what you need to change to make your heart right with Him. If you are fashion conscious, use this tendency to remind you to search your heart before the Lord.

DAY 5: Psalm 130:1-4

Out of the depths I cry to you, O Lord; O Lord, hear my voice. Let your ears be attentive to my cry for mercy. If you, O Lord kept a record of sins, O Lord, who could stand? But with you there is forgiveness; therefore you are feared.

Now and then if you are reading the Psalms, you will see beneath the numbers these words: "a song of ascent." Here is what this notation is referring to: when the Israelites would go up to Jerusalem to worship, they had to climb a hill. You will always hear about "going up to Jerusalem" because Jerusalem is built on a hill, and no matter what direction you are coming from, you have to climb this hill to get to the city. So, when the Israelites were coming to the temple to worship, to celebrate the feasts, and to bring sacrifices, they would sing. They sang these special psalms to prepare their hearts to confess their sins while they were going to worship. Picture a family walking along the dusty roads, singing this song. Picture yourself singing this song on the way to church, crying out to God for forgiveness, praising His mercy. Notice the response the psalmist gives to the forgiveness of God: fear. This simply means astonished reverence. One of the things that happens to us when we see God's forgiveness is that we realize that we don't deserve it, and instead deserve punishment. That's when we are going to be amazed at Him.

Write your own "song of ascent" to sing or read on your way to worship. It doesn't have to be poetic, just express your love and reverence for God and confess your sins.

_____
_____
_____
_____
_____

DAY 6: Proverbs 7:2-3

Keep my commands and you will live; guard my teachings as the apple of your eye. Bind them on your fingers; write them on the tablet of your heart.

If you hadn't noticed it already, humans are forgetful. You don't have to wait until you are old to start losing track of names, details, and appointments. Sometimes this isn't such a big deal, but there is one place where it really matters. We can't afford to forget God's commands. We can't afford to let the teachings of His word slip away from us. We have to remember them. When you are in school, and listening to a lecture, you say, "This is going to be on the test. I have got to remember it. I will write this down." Writing things down is a great way to remember them. Number one, the more ways you process a piece of information, the more likely you are to remember it. This is simple brain function. Number two, if you have it written down, you can refer back to it later. You have more chances to memorize the information. When we are listening to God's Word being expounded upon, we have to treat it like this. We have to process the information and remember it, because there is going to be a big test. We are going to have to apply this to our lives. Taking notes on paper is a good start. But this is so important that we have to take it further. We have to internalize it. We have to take notes on our hearts.

One of the best ways to take "heart notes" is to memorize and meditate on scripture. Try it this week. Pick one verse to learn, and spend a little time each day meditating upon it.

_____
_____
_____
_____
_____

DAY 7: Psalm 98:1, 4

Sing to the LORD a new song, for he has done marvelous things; his right hand and his holy arm have worked salvation for him. ... Shout for joy to the LORD, all the earth, burst into jubilant song with music.

It is interesting to note that throughout church history, every time there has been a great spiritual awakening it has been accompanied by new music. There is something about that first rush of joy that produces a special kind of spontaneous praise to the Lord. The book of Revelation tells us that we will be singing a new song when we get to heaven. The Lord likes to hear new songs of praise from our mouths. The problem is, most of us are not song writers. We do not regularly write new songs to the Lord. This does not mean that we cannot "sing a new song." Neither does it mean that we cannot enjoy and reuse the rich musical heritage that the church has. It has to do with how we sing the songs. Do you sing the words of a familiar song while your mind is a million miles away? Or do you think about the words, and make them your own, using them to personally praise God? If you sing a song one hundred times, and each time it is spontaneous praise to the Lord and you mean every word; then it is a like a new song of worship each time.

Singing new songs to the Lord in your own words is great, too. Even if you can't sing, you can shout! Write in your own words a "new song" of praise.

_____
_____
_____
_____
_____
_____

DAY 8: 1 Timothy 6: 17-18

Command those who are rich in the present world not to be arrogant nor to put their hope in wealth, which is so uncertain, but to put their hope in God, who richly provides us with everything for our enjoyment. Command them to do good, to be rich in good deeds, and to be generous and willing to share.

Do you ever wonder why God gives us an abundance of material goods? It is not just so that we can live in opulence. God gives us extra so that we can have the privilege of giving generously. If we take our material goods, hoard them, and rely on them for security and satisfaction, we are going to be missing out on one of God's great blessings. We sometimes become "clutchers," afraid to let go of our money or things, imagining that God is a killjoy who doesn't want us to have anything nice. This is so wrong! God richly provides for us, including "everything for our enjoyment." The lesson we have to learn is that we only get this when we let go and give it all back to Him.

This teaching is not just for those with extra. God wants us all to give, trusting in Him for our physical needs as well as spiritual needs. If you ever start thinking "Well, I would give, but I don't have enough money," take a look at this verse: "Out of the most severe trial, their overflowing joy and their extreme poverty welled up in rich generosity." (2 Corinthians 8:2).

Read Matthew 6:19-24. Where do you think you have the most treasure stored up?

_____
_____
_____
_____
_____

DAY 9: James 1:22

Do not merely listen to the word, and so deceive yourselves. Do what it says.

When we have made the commitment to come to the corporate worship services, when we are writing it down, singing it up and giving it out, we still have one very important function we have to perform. If we are not living it, all the rest will not do us a particle of good. We have to learn to be sponges, to absorb and internalize what we hear; we have to apply it and work it out practically in our lives. When we are just listening, we can easily agree with what the preacher is saying. We can hear the words of the songs, and say, "Oh, yes, that is a good song. What a nice thing for that person to sing." We can say, "Oh, that was a good sermon. That doctrine is really what the Bible says. I know about six people who should have heard this message," and yet we never apply it to ourselves. We feel good because we agreed with all the right stuff. We feel spiritual because we attend a church that has such great sermons. But we are deceived. Merely listening will get us nowhere. We have to do what it says. Real spirituality is lived out in a changed life, not just discussed over coffee and doughnuts or listened to on Sunday morning.

What is your ratio between listening and doing? What one thing do you think you should work on applying to your life right now?

DAY 10: Colossians 4:5

Be wise in the way you act toward outsiders; make the most of every opportunity.

Part of the reason for learning to be really engaged in the weekly worship service is just for us. When we are prepared and participating we will gain so much more and grow so much more that we would be crazy not to make the most of it.

We should also be engaged because God is worthy of the respect of undivided attention. We have an appointment with the great and holy God of the Universe. We are not going to show up late and yawn through it, and then walk off without remembering a word that was said. If we do that, we are in bad shape. We are really missing something.

A third reason for being engaged in worship, both in church and outside of it is because of the people who are watching. We are the ambassadors of Christ here on this earth, and it is our job to portray Him to unbelievers. When they see us worshipping with our lives through the week, making God our priority, preparing for and looking forward to corporate worship; then they will see that this is something for real. This is life changing. This church thing must really do something for people. What is your witness like?

What did you see in the lives of believers that attracted you to Christianity? Do you think that you are portraying this to the unbelievers around you now?

THE FINEST HOUR

SESSION FIVE

Hebrews 10:25

You smile with satisfaction when you read your e-mail because you finally secured that meeting with the man who can change the course of your career. The meeting is set for the next day at 8:00 a.m. in his office. The night before, you go through all of the preparations. You get your sales pitch down cold. You run through the different scenarios. You try to predict the questions that he will ask. You pick just the right clothes to wear. You get a good night's rest. You arrive early for the appointment and his assistant escorts you into his palatial office. You settle in one of those butter-soft leather chairs. You lock eyes with him and you can feel in your gut that great things are going to happen. The conversation flows and there is a real connection during the meeting. He gives you several insightful suggestions that you quickly hammer out on your laptop. Money is discussed and a contract is drawn up on the spot. You shake hands and leave. The deal has been done. It has been your finest hour in the marketplace, and your career will never be the same. There is nothing like those meetings that matter, is there?

Start It Up

Even if you are not a big business tycoon, you have undoubtedly had an appointment that was very important to you. It may not have even had anything to do with money—for instance, it may have been a first date or a meeting with a physician who told you something that profoundly affected your life.

1. Share with the group about a meeting in your life that was important to you. What happened?

Talk It Up

We are directed to live a life of worship. We have to be mirrors that reflect God's glory. We should be committed to worship all the time. We also have a standing appointment with the God of the universe, the true power broker. When we show up and do business with Him, a cosmic transaction takes place. Every time we leave church, we should be launched onto a new level. It should change the very course of our lives. There is something special about corporate worship, and we can't afford to neglect it.

Read Hebrews 10:25

We are not to let a little bad weather, a little excuse, a little sports game or anything else get in the way of our corporate meeting with God. When we turn our backs on church attendance, when we don't regularly worship Him with other believers, we are ditching one of God's most basic directives. We are rejecting an opportunity to do business with Him.

2. **What excuses are likely to keep you away from church? How committed are you to coming every week?**

Preparation

We need to make the commitment to come to church, but there is more to it than that. When we think about corporate worship, we have to think about preparation. We have to be prepared for worship. Hold out your hand right now and look at it. We have five things that we need to do to be prepared for worship, that's one for each finger.

Take your thumb first. It stands for the fact that we should be **rested up**. In other words, preparation for Sunday worship begins on Saturday. We should get a good night's rest. If we aren't prepared in this way, then when we get to church on Sunday morning, we are going to be a lot more interested in finding the softest chair than in meeting with God. We are going to be propping our eyelids up with toothpicks instead of sitting on the edges of our seats listening to what He has to say to us.

The pointer finger stands for being **prayed up**. Do you pray before you come to church? We have learned throughout this study that if we know Christ personally, everything we do and say should be an act of worship. If you are a Christ follower, you should pray regularly. You need to be praying for the leaders of the church, the people of the church, and the behind the scenes workers at church. Pray for those who come who don't know Christ. Pray that the believers will ratchet up their behavior; they will take a character step and really understand the true implications of going deeper with God. You have got to be rested up and prayed up.

Your tallest finger stands for **heads up**. Treat going to church as a priority, not something that you might get to later, if you get around to it. Would you do this if a billionaire said, "Meet me at 12 noon at such and such a restaurant, and I will give you a million dollars"? If you got that kind of invitation, you would be there early. You would not say, "I'll just push this to the wire, and if I make it fine, if not, fine." Get up, get there, and take it all in. Don't just walk in halfway through to listen to your favorite part of the service. What about walking out before the service is over? What is the big rush? Isn't Sunday supposed to be a day of rest? "Well, I am going to win the race to the nearest hamburger joint. I have to get there first." Since when has a burger been more important than your appointment with God?

Take your ring finger. This is a tricky one. It stands for **dressing up**. Don't you love getting dressed up? It is great to look your best and to show honor to God by coming to your appointment looking good. But the downside of this is that it is easy for us humans to turn dressing nicely for church into a fashion show. It can become a time for showing off to each other, rather than focusing on the Lord. It is also true that our culture is a casual culture. Many people don't feel comfortable dressed up. Many people have to be dressed up all week, and love to have a chance to dress casually. One of the reasons to dress casually is to show that you can come to church just like you are, wearing casual clothes. Jesus loves you just the way you are, just the way you look. We have got to think through being dressed up. Think about your appointment with God. Dress in such a way that you show respect, but don't let it become your focus. Don't let it become a fashion contest.

The last finger, the pinkie, stands for being **'fessed up**. We need to confess our sins and come clean before the Lord. We have got to have a clean slate before we can worship Him. If we are smudged and marred by all the times we messed up this week, we are not going to be able to reflect God's majesty. We are not going to be able to focus on Him or be passionate about Him. So, we have got to confess. We have got to humbly acknowledge who we really are, and ask God for forgiveness.

3. Which of these areas of worship preparation do you struggle with the most? What can you do to become better in this area?

4. What do you think might be the results of greater preparation for the corporate worship service? Why?

Participation

We have got the hand of worship down cold. We understand the importance of preparation. Now let's change gears and talk about participation. Just imagine this scenario: you are in church, and everything is going on as usual. Then your pastor tells you that he has a special guest here this morning. Everyone waits with bated breath to hear who this special guest is. As the drum rolls the pastor introduces your favorite celebrity. This person comes out on stage and the crowd goes wild. The pastor then turns the rest of the service over to the celebrity and everyone instantly becomes engaged in the message— listening intently from then on. Wait, wait, wait! What is going on here? All of a sudden, we are engaged because we have a celebrity guest? Do you realize that every single week we have the most important guest of all? Every week Jesus Christ is in the service with us. Do we have the level of participation for Him that we would have for a Hollywood celebrity?

Well, how do we participate in worship? **Write it down**. Start by taking notes. We have a very depressing statistic out there. Did you know that you forget 95% of what you hear on Sunday morning by Wednesday? On Wednesday you will be walking around saying, "I can remember this one little tidbit, but I can't remember what it connected to." That is a real downer. But if you write it down, you would be amazed at what you will remember. Get yourself a notebook, and make it into your weekend teaching journal. Take notes, jot down references, and outline the message. Write down your prayer requests and the answers God gives. Write down what you learn in your personal devotions. There is something special about writing things down.

Point of Action

You have just been challenged to do something in the previous paragraph. Do you remember what it was? If you have already forgotten it is just proof that you really need to do it. The challenge was to start being a participant in worship by keeping a written record. Go to a store today and buy something you can use as a worship journal; it can be a 99 cent spiral notebook or a nicely bound leather book. It doesn't matter what you use just as long as you use it. Take it to worship services and make notes from the message, journal your prayers and how God answers them, record references to Scripture. Ratchet up your worship by becoming a participant.

5. Note-taking is just a part of listening skills. How good are you at listening? What strategies can you think of to improve your listening?

Don't just write it down; also **sing it up**. Seventeen times the Bible says to sing to the Lord, not just about Him. Sing to the Lord. It doesn't matter whether you are musical or not, whether you have a great voice or can even carry a tune. God wants to hear our voices. Sing unashamedly to God.

After we sing it up, we are to do something else. We are to **give it out**. Yes, you can give without worshipping, but you can't worship without giving. God is so gracious to include us in His economic plan. Think about it. We use our energy, our creativity, our discipline, and our vision to make money. Money is a means of exchange. And when we give to the local church, we are giving a part of ourselves. We are tangibly saying that God is the Lord of it all.

Read Proverbs 3:9-12.

Notice that directly after the Lord talks about money in this passage, He talks about discipline. Why did God talk about discipline following money? God knew that we would struggle with it. When you just throw a bone God's way, just pocket change, one day you will be disciplined. This is not to scare you. It is just a fact that one day you will stand before God and He will ask how you handled your finances.

6. How much do you think you should be giving? What kinds of blessings have you experienced through giving?

When we participate in worship, we also have to **soak it in**: "Lord, I want to be a sponge today. I want to soak it in. I want to soak in the music, soak in the drama, soak in everything." It's great if we leave church saying, "Wow, that was a great solo! She sure is an incredible singer. Wow, that drama team is wonderful! Doesn't the pastor tell the funniest stories you have ever heard?" All those things are fine and good, but they should not be our first response. Our first response should be application. We should ask, "How did the song deal with my character? How did the drama pose a question or give an illustration that set the stage for the message? What should I do because of what I was given this weekend?"

7. What practical tips can you think of to become good "sponges"?

Practice
This leads us to the next thing we are going to talk about. Practice. We have got to practice it. Think about this question. Can something be irrelevant and true? You better believe it! Just imagine that you have injured yourself badly. You are rushed to the emergency room, and a couple of doctors walk up to you. You know you are in trouble when the doctors say, "You really messed up, man! You must be in intense pain." The doctor is not going to lean over you and say, "Do you know what pain is? Well let me give you a word study on this word 'pain.' Pain comes from two Latin words…" He is not going to tell you that you are in a hospital, and that you should know the history of the hospital before you are checked in. No, those things would be true, but they would not be relevant. The doctor is going to say, "You are messed up. Here is some pain-killer. Here is the surgeon." That is what we have to do in the local church. For far too long the church has been long on diagnosis but short on remedy. And it has been disobedient to Christ's model. Two-thirds of

Christ's words were words of application, words of relevancy, words of shoe leather. We are to walk it out in our lives. We have to be a life application church, because Jesus and the Bible are all about applying God's truth to our lives.

8. In what ways have you found the worship service enhanced by the participation and preparation of those around you? What is a "truth" that you have recently put into practice in your life?

Lift It Up

The real measure of a church is what happens in people's lives between services. We have talked about the hours of our week. We only have about two hours of corporate worship, only two hours to encourage and teach and strengthen each other. During those two hours at church, we better bust it. We had better be prepared. We had better be participating. And we had better be practicing what we learn. This is the time to be strengthened and encouraged, the time to get ready to worship the other 110 hours of the week. We worship more outside the church than in the church. When we have that down: the preparation, the participation, and the practice; we will understand what it means to be fully engaged in the finest hour.

9. What needs do you think of, in your own life, in the lives of other believers, or in the lives of your leaders that you can pray for in preparation for next Sunday?

Take time to pray for one another.

MY PRAYER REQUESTS

_____
_____
_____
_____
_____
_____
_____
_____
_____
_____
_____

MY GROUP'S PRAYER REQUESTS

_____
_____
_____
_____
_____
_____
_____
_____
_____
_____
_____
_____
_____
_____
_____
_____
_____

THE FINEST HOUR

DAY 1: Romans 12:1

Therefore, I urge you brothers in view of God's mercy to offer your bodies as living sacrifices, holy and pleasing to God which is your spiritual act of worship.

Have you realized by now that worship is a lifestyle? It is not something that we can keep in a neat little box for Sunday morning. In the Old Testament, a lot of people thought that God resided in the tabernacle, and later the temple. While it is true that He did manifest His presence there in a special way, Jesus made it clear in the New Testament that God is not confined to a building. Then He added that we are the house, if we receive and know Him. Worship is not some compartmentalized thing that you do on Saturday, or Sunday, or in a home group meeting, or in men's or women's Bible study. Worship is a lifestyle. This text in Romans is saying that wherever we are, whomever we are with, anytime, any place, worship should be going on. We can come to church and shed tears and lift our hands and kneel and sing to God. But if worship does not involve life change, transcend into your marriage or dating relationship, into your parenting skills, into your priorities, thoughts, activities, vocabulary, into the places you go, then it is not really worship. It is just a compartmentalized thing. Jesus said, "If you love Me, you are to keep My commandments." Christianity is not some legalistic trip. Each of us should live a holy, pleasing, and sacrifice-driven life before God. That should be our spiritual act of worship. We should be intensely passionate about the person of Christ.

Have you ever consciously offered yourself, body, soul and spirit, to God as a sacrifice? Think of the altar in the temple, and mentally crawl up on it. Tell God that you want to be dedicated wholly to Him.

_____

_____

_____

DAY 2: Revelation 1:16b-18

...His face was like the sun shining in all its brilliance. When I saw him, I fell at his feet as though dead. Then he placed his right hand on me and said: "Do not be afraid. I am the First and the Last. I am the Living One; I was dead, and behold I am alive for ever and ever! And I hold the keys of death and Hades."

Worship can't be compartmentalized. It can't be kept safely in one little box in our lives. No, when we worship, we are going to be changed. Sometimes this hurts. Sometimes this can be scary. We are going to find that God's presence will penetrate us to the very depths, and we aren't going to like what He finds there. When we are engaged in worship, we are coming face-to-face with God, and when we come face to face with God, we come face to face with His holiness. When we are standing in the blaze of His glory, we are going to see ourselves the way we really are. We will see that we are covered in dirt. We are not worthy to come before Him. We will be scared. In fact, John was so scared he fainted. The good news is Jesus' response. He reached out and touched John. Listen to what He said: "Don't be afraid." We can stand before the Holy God in all our imperfections, and not fear. He made us. He loved us and bought us. And He is making us over into His image.

Is worship still in a safe box in your life? Or are you letting God's presence penetrate to the secret places? Ask God to let you see His glory. It will hurt, because you have to see yourself as well. But it will be worth it.

_/_____
_/_____
_/_____
_/_____
_/_____
_/_____

DAY 3: Romans 14:10-11

You, then, why do you judge your brother? Or why do you look down on your brother? For we will all stand before God's judgment seat. It is written: "As surely as I live," says the Lord, "Every knee will bow before me; every tongue will confess to God."

When God's presence penetrates, perspective changes. When we live a life of worship, it will alter the way we look at one another. When we are kneeling before God, worshipping Him, we are focused on Him only. There is no room to look around at everyone else, comparing and rating them. We will only see ourselves before God. And when we see ourselves before God, we realize how unworthy we are. In light of this, how can we look down our noses at others? The time will come when they will have to bow before the Lord at the judgment seat, and He will deal with all their shortcomings—as He will deal with each one of us. The more time we spend worshipping God, the less time we will have to be critical of our brothers and sisters. When we worship, the playing field is leveled. We can see that not one of us is a cut above the others, not one has an advantage with more natural holiness, or less sin-nature.

What can you do to clear from your mind the critical and self-praising thoughts about other believers?

_____

_____

_____

_____

_____

_____

_____

_____

_____

DAY 4: Psalm 100:1-2

Shout for joy to the Lord, all the earth. Worship the Lord with gladness; come before him with joyful songs. Know that the Lord is God. It is he who made us, and we are his; we are his people, the sheep of his pasture.

Worship is not a passive thing, it is an active thing. We live in a spectator driven society, don't we? We look at things other people are doing and rate them. We channel surf through life. If we get bored watching one thing, we switch to something else. We have to have someone entertaining us all the time.

Listen to the active words in this psalm: Shout. Worship. Come. Sing. Know. Worship is active. Read the rest of Psalm 100, and note the other active words: Enter. Give. Praise. God deserves your worship. Also, you desperately need it. Every time you worship, it will put you in the right place with your priorities right. You realize that God is God and you are not. There is a popular god out there that all of us struggle with as far as worship goes—ourselves. We are probably God's biggest competition. Worship is not about us, it is about God.

Read Psalm 95, and write down all the action words in this psalm of worship.

_____

_____

_____

_____

_____

_____

_____

_____

DAY 5: Matthew 4:8-10

Again, the devil took him to a very high mountain and showed him all the kingdoms of the world and their splendor. "All this I will give you," he said, "if you will bow down and worship me." Jesus said to him, "Away from me, Satan! For it is written: "'Worship the Lord your God, and serve him only.'"

Satan came to our Lord after He had fasted forty days and forty nights and said, "Jesus, you are hungry. Turn these stones into bread." Jesus said, "I am not going there." Then Satan said, "Let's fly up to the top of the temple and once there you can throw yourself down and the angels will rescue you." Jesus said, "I am not going there either." Finally, Satan came to his real point. He turned up the volume. He took our Lord to a mountain range and said, "Check out the world. All of this can be yours, Jesus, if you bow down and worship me." What did Jesus say? Read the verse again. Only one is worthy of worship. You know, it is always the same in our lives. Whatever Satan is doing, he is trying to turn our worship away from God—he will try to lure you to worship himself, to worship materialism, to worship anything. He promises us the world if we will turn away from God, but he is promising something he does not own. The world belongs to God, and Satan can't give it to anyone. Don't let him fool you. There is only One worthy of worship.

When have you been fooled into turning your focus onto the wrong things? What was promised? What really happened? What can you do to change your focus back to God right now?

_____
_____
_____
_____
_____

DAY 6: Ephesians 6:13

Therefore put on the full armor of God, so that when the day of evil comes, you may be able to stand your ground, and after you have done everything, to stand.

Satan is highly motivated to mess up our worship. If he can't get our souls, he'd like to keep us from reflecting God's glory. He'd like to keep us from filling our lives with worship. Sometimes he works by distractions, sometimes by direct attacks, but his aim is always the same: he wants to keep us from being true worshippers. He wants our hearts to be turned towards him, towards materialism, pleasure, revenge, hatred, greed, fear, romance, towards anything but worshipping God. As we become true worshippers, learning to worship with the whole of our life and self, we will have a heightened awareness of God's presence. We will know Him better, and as we learn to know Him better He will make us more like Him. At the same time, we become prey of greater interest to the Evil One. As we grow closer to God, allowing worship to open up our lives and clean us out, the warfare will increase. We have to be prepared for battle, and that means getting up every morning and buckling on our armor. God has provided us with all we need to withstand the fiery darts of the Enemy. But we have to put it on.

Read the next few verses in this passage (Eph. 6:13-18). Write down at least one practical application/interpretation for each of the pieces of armor mentioned. How can you "put on" this "armor" today?

_____

_____

_____

_____

_____

_____

DAY 7: Psalm 103:1

Praise the LORD, O my soul; all my inmost being, praise his holy name.

When we become serious about being real worshippers, all the dividing lines in our lives are going to be washed away. We can't keep worship for a certain day, or a certain time, or use only one section of our brains, or let God see one corner of our hearts. No, when worship begins to be a part of our lives it is going to push through the walls. It will seep all the way into our inmost beings. God wants us to worship Him in our very essence, in the very core of the self. He wants to be the one we instinctively turn to first before we even get to the point of conscious thought. He knows us through and through, even to the most secret place in the heart. He is worthy of all our worship.

How do you respond to the knowledge that the God we are worshipping is holy? Have you invited Him into your "secret places"?

DAY 8: Acts 5:40b-41

They called the apostles in and had them flogged. Then they ordered them not to speak in the name of Jesus, and let them go. The apostles left the Sanhedrin, rejoicing because they had been counted worthy of suffering disgrace for the Name.

They sound crazy, don't they? Here they have just been beaten brutally and ordered to quit talking about Jesus, and they come out rejoicing? On the face of it, it just doesn't make sense, but this is what can happen in a life characterized by worship. When we practice turning every experience into an opportunity to bring praise to God, we start to see things from His perspective. It gives us a new take on trials. Instead of looking just at the surface, at the pain or inconvenience or humiliation or sorrow, we can look deeper. However dimly, we know that there is more to it than meets the eye. We know that He is in control, and even though it is tough, we can trust Him. As we turn our lives into worship, it means that we are thinking about Him all the time. As we think about Him, praise Him and talk to Him, we draw closer and closer to Him. The closer we get, the better we learn to know Him. He talks back to us. He teaches us. He molds us into His own image. And we learn to trust Him and continue to worship. Then, when the trials come, we can rejoice.

What trials are in your life now? How are you responding to them? How should you respond?

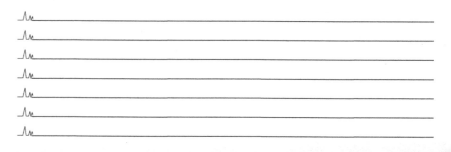

DAY 9: Matthew 26:6-7

While Jesus was in Bethany in the home of a man known as Simon the Leper, a woman came to him with an alabaster jar of very expensive perfume, which she poured on his head as he was reclining at the table.

It must have looked really weird to the rest of the company. After all, is it normal to pour perfume all over your guests at the dinner table? Besides, that was some cash she was wasting. The disciples were disgusted. That perfume could have been sold for a lot of money—to be used for a good cause of course. She should have given it to the poor. They started to scold her for her foolishness. But Jesus put a stop to that. He did not call her action weird or bad. Instead, he said, "She has done a beautiful thing to me." Beautiful. She loved Him so much, she thought only of Jesus. She did not even see the rest of the crowd. She didn't care that they would think she was strange. All she thought of was worshipping Him with her sweet perfume.

Only Jesus. Are your eyes on Him? Would you walk through a crowd of people who thought you were nuts, to offer Him the perfume of your worship? Is He first and foremost in your life? Is He before making a little profit—even for a good cause? Is He before "someone might think I am weird"? Every single thing we do should be for Him, because of Him, in Him, through Him. That is living worship.

Do you want to be this close to Jesus? Start by asking Him to remind you to think of Him. The more you practice turning your thoughts to the Lord, the easier it will become. Make a commitment also to read from His Word each day, and think about what you read.

_____

_____

_____

DAY 10: Revelation 22:3-4

No longer will there be any curse. The throne of God and of the Lamb will be in the city, and his servants will serve him. They will see his face, and his name will be on their foreheads.

Ultimately, when we graduate from this life to the next, we become quintessential worshippers. That means that we will be purely and perfectly God worshippers. Scripture says that those of us who know Christ, whose names are written in the Lamb's book of life, will go to heaven. Every glimpse of heaven in the Bible is a glimpse of worship. We are not talking about some giant worship service where you have a pipe organ or a worship team, and a pastor preaches on and on through all eternity. We are talking about a place where the curse is lifted, and every activity, thought, and goal will be perfect. Everything we do will have behind it the passion of praise and worship to our God.

What is the nearest to a "glimpse of heaven" that you have seen on this earth?

WRAPPING IT UP

SESSION SIX

Gifts are fun. We all like them. We like to think about them, buy them, wrap them, and unwrap them. But you know, the stuff we get and give over our lives will go out of style. It will rust, quit working, or get used up. But God has a different kind of gift for us: the gift of worship. It is a gift that literally keeps on giving. It plays out in this life and the next. You may ask, "Present? Gift? Worship can be talked about in these terms?" The answer is a resounding "Yes!" God has given us all the opportunity to know Him personally through Christ. Once we make that decision, once that cosmic transaction takes place, everything in our lives should be about worship. Today, as we wrap up this whole process, we are going to talk about utilizing the gift of worship.

Start It Up

A good gift does not have to be an object. Sometimes the best gifts we can receive are kind actions or simply the knowledge that someone loves us.

1. **Share with the group the most meaningful non-material gift you have received from another person.**

Talk It Up

Everything we do and think should be an act of worship. Worship should transcend every facet of our lives. That is what Scripture tells us. If you make the choice to know Christ personally, to show your incredible relationship with Him in everything you do, say, and touch, then it will transform your life.

Think back to your kindergarten days, when you had those little cubbyholes to put your stuff in. Your cubbyhole was your space, your compartment. Most of us, without even realizing it, compartmentalize or cubbyhole our lives. We have the different parts of our lives set up so that they don't touch each other.

We say, "My activities are here, my finances are there, my career is in this section, and my relationships are in that section." We love cubbyholes. And we have God confined and defined in a little cubbyhole, too. We go to church, bow the knee, and worship Him. Then we jump into the car and leave, leaving God at church in His little cubbyhole. This can't last. Real biblical worship, means that while God is active, real and alive at church, He should also transcend every part of our lives. To worship is to become intensely passionate about the person of Jesus Christ. It is mirroring the majesty of the Maker in everything. If we just do the cubbyhole thing, we are missing out on the transforming power of worship.

Read Isaiah 6:5

The power of worship is constructive. It will transform and build us into mirrors of Christ. But the power of worship is also destructive. It is not always pleasant. If we are really serious about worship, it will be like taking a chainsaw to our cubbyhole system. It will cut through the dividing walls we have set up in our lives. It will transcend everything else. It means that our activities, finances, career, and relationships will all be free of their cubicles. It means that we can't keep God in the "Sunday mornings only" compartment. He will become a part of all we do, say, and think. Trying to cubbyhole God will never work. We will never be what we are wired to be until we understand that we are wired for worship. We must allow worship to transcend every aspect of our lives.

Discernment

When we actually unwrap the gift of worship and apply it in our lives, here is what will happen. Worship will deepen our discernment. Talk to people who have allowed worship to do the chainsaw thing and you'll see that they are people who have a deep level of discernment. Discernment includes several things. First of all, we are going to talk about the **hygiene issue**. Look again at what Scripture has to say about our hygiene in Isaiah 6:5. Do you notice the recurring theme "unclean"? Unclean. This is what the lepers were supposed to shout, to keep people at a distance and prevent the spread of their disease. While Isaiah was worshipping God, God revealed Himself and Isaiah saw himself in the blaze of God's glory. He saw how dirty he really was. Isaiah was unclean, and aware of his situation. The scary thing is when we are unclean and unaware. We can be covered in filth, and be totally oblivious. Often, we think that we have to do something bad to mess up our fellowship with God. It is true, "big sins" will mess up our fellowship, but realize that we can have a major hygiene problem without ever actually doing anything. We can be unclean in our thoughts. God wants to dwell in our thoughts, but how can He dwell in polluted thoughts, toxic thoughts, materialistic thoughts, selfish thoughts, lustful thoughts, or greed-driven thoughts?

Read Proverbs 28:13.

2. Since God knows all that we do and think anyway, why are we told to not conceal sins from Him?

3. When have you experienced the kind of mercy this verse talks about?

Discernment is also a **priority thing**. It affects our priorities. Look at someone who has great priorities, and you will see someone who is a person of worship. People are always saying, "Well, I am just so busy. I am going here. I am going there. I am going everywhere!" It is so laughable when you ask people these days how they are doing and their response is that they are busy. In other words, that means they are important.

People who are worshippers understand how to simplify their lives. They understand where church fits in. They understand that they should orbit their lives around the local church. They understand the relational aspect of priorities, God first, then spouse, and finally family. They understand that career comes in about fourth. They have a grasp on the fact that God has included us in His economic plan and they give generously. In activities they only do things that mirror the majesty of their maker.

Point of Action

Re-read the order of priorities in the previous paragraph. Does your life reflect this order or are you one of the millions of people today who have misplaced their priorities? If you are not sure how you have prioritized your life try this: keep a record for one week of where you spend your time, your money, and your energy. This might seem a little extreme, but try it for just one week. At the end of seven days tally the time, money and energy spent of each in these three areas of your life: God, family, and work. Are you in a priority predicament? Are your priorities way out of whack? Maybe you are like most people and just need some small priority tweaks for your life to reach higher peaks. Do whatever it takes to get your life properly prioritized and do it as an act of worship to God.

4. How high a priority is worship in your life right now? How have you seen your priorities change as you understand more about worship?

It is also a **perception thing**. People who worship have a deeper perception of spiritual truth. During daily devotional time, words leap off the pages of Scripture. When they come to church they perceive how God is working and moving. When they ratchet up their worship they will experience an increase of spiritual warfare.

When we really get serious about worship, the evil one will take steps to get after us. You know why? Every time we worship, every time we do the chainsaw thing, it reminds the evil one of his former job. Lucifer used to lead worship in heaven. One day, though, he made the decision to try and blow God out of the way and have every bit of worship come to himself. Due to his rebellion, God tossed Lucifer out of heaven along with a third of the angelic beings who now make up the demonic realm in our world today. When we begin to chainsaw areas of our lives, letting worship flow into every area; the spiritual warfare increases. When you unwrap the gift of worship, it will deepen your discernment.

Read Hebrews 13:15.

Thankfulness

Worship will help us to have a new take on our trials. Trials will happen, big trials, medium trials and small trials. And this flies right in the face of people of faith. In Hebrews 13:15, did you notice that word, "continually"? Wow. We have no problem worshipping God and mirroring the majesty of our Maker when life is a steady stream of superlatives, when the family is healthy, wealthy and wise. No problem. Twenty-four seven, "I love you, Lord." But, what happens when we are suddenly faced with difficult times?

Read Psalm 34:1.

David said, "at all times," and "always." How in the world can we do this? How can we feel worshipful and thankful no matter what comes down the pike? Is that the deal, to have a phony, fake, "Praise the Lord, I am ready for another trial—bring it on"? No, not that phony mumbo jumbo junk. This is a decision. We have to choose, as a matter of obedience, to give thanks in everything, trials, or good days. We are to worship God, to mirror the majesty of our Maker in everything.

We are not talking about feelings. God is not telling us to feel feelings of thanksgiving when we are facing trials. We can't drum up a feeling of worship when we are facing adverse circumstances or situations. Feelings are not reliable. They are affected by a poor round at the golf course. They are affected by an argument, by the weather, or by illness. We can't always control our feelings, but we can control our actions. Thanking God for trials is a decision that we make. We can say, no matter how we feel, "God, I don't understand, and I don't like it, but I am making the decision to thank You for it, because You said to. I want to mirror You. Help me to understand this, to accept this, to learn from this. Thank You."

If you haven't noticed, you are in an aquarium and the people around you have their faces pressed up against the glass. They want to see how you are doing life deeply with God. They want to see what will happen when the wrecking ball smashes the aquarium.

5. **Read Acts 16:22-34. Discuss the part that worship played in this drama.**

6. **When have you undergone a serious trial that you had a hard time thanking God for? How did you handle this?**

Lift It Up

Listen to Psalm 22:3 in the King James Version. "But thou art holy, oh thou that inhabitest the praises of Israel." In other words, worship is where God lives. It is His address. So, if we want God to be at home in our lives we had better be involved in worship. While God is everywhere—that is His quality of omnipresence—God is manifested to a greater degree when those who love Him, worship Him.

Over the last six weeks we have discussed worship extensively. Let's not let it stop there. Unwrap the gift of worship, the gift of discernment, the gift that gives us a new take on trials, the gift that opens up our lives to the deeper manifestation of God's presence. Worship Him with your whole life.

7. How has this study impacted you? In what area of your life do you feel that you have the hardest time worshipping? How can this group pray for you and encourage you?

Take time to pray for one another

MY PRAYER REQUESTS

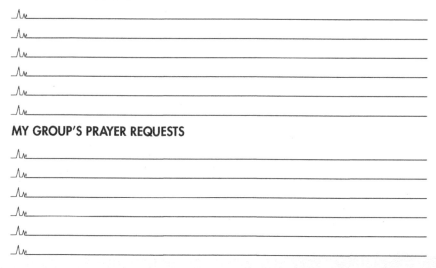

MY GROUP'S PRAYER REQUESTS

WIRED FOR WORSHIP LEADER'S GUIDE

Session One : Introduction

In what way would you define the word "worship"? What would you add to the description given above?

A: Use the description given in the text for a reference. Also use a dictionary definition for the word to compare and contrast the different ways people perceive worship. Remember there is no "right" answer; these are opinions.

"God is not served by human hands, as if he needed anything." Why does He want us to worship Him?

A: Our worship is the ultimate expression of our love and thankfulness to a worthy God. It is also a means to ensure that we keep our focus on Him. It is for our own good.

What does it mean that, "in him we live and move and have our being"?

A: God is the Creator and we are His creation. Without Him we have nothing; we are nothing. Looking at Acts 17:26 Paul says that God has a plan and a purpose for each of us all the way to the point where He plans our time on earth and where we will live.

Why did God overlook ignorance about worship in the past? What has changed so that He is demanding repentance now?

A: Before this time God overlooked the worship ignorance of unknowing people because they were unknowing. Only the Jews of the day were educated about worshipping God. Once Jesus' ministry began, the door was opened for everyone and the ignorance excuse was forever erased.

What will be the consequence of failing to worship God?

A: Stunted Christian growth marked by a less-than-fruitful life.

Session Two : Style vs. Substance

What is the significance of the argument about worship location? When have you dealt with this kind of argument?

A: The argument centers around worship being confined to a certain location versus being an "all-the-time, everywhere thing."

Was Jesus' response a change or a clarification of God's original worship requirements?

A: Discuss both sides of this question because Jesus' statement both clarified God's plan for worship and introduced a change. God has always intended for worship to be a lifestyle. (See 1 Samuel 15:22) In Old Testament times God also gave very specific instructions on corporate worship that could only be carried out within the temple. Once Jesus came as the final sacrifice, the Old Testament worship requirements were no longer applicable. Today we are free to worship God any time, any place.

How can you tell for sure if you are hearing from the Holy Spirit, especially about issues that don't seem to be clearly defined in Scripture? Share with the group from your experiences in being guided by the Holy Spirit.

A: Remember to let people share their experiences, but look for the common threads of personal conviction, the power of prayer, the seeking of wise counsel, listening for God's answer, and Scriptural support.

Session Three : 110 Hours of Worship

What are some things that keep you from worshipping 110 hours every week?

A: Answers might include the obvious distractions – work, television, the busyness of life, etc. Raise the possibility that perhaps we do not know how to worship on an every day basis or that we simply do not know the need for it.

Where are you now on your "mountain of worship"?

A: Regardless of a person's answer to this question be sure that you are an encouragement to them.

Session Four : The Ultimate Introduction

What does the name I AM tell us about God?

A: The name I AM reflects the unchanging nature of our Holy God–He has always been, is today, and always will be.

How should knowing these four different names of God affect the way we respond to Him?

A: These four names and what they tell us about the character and the nature of God should cause us to respond to Him with a very real fear –and this word means "astonished reverence"–of God.

Session Five : The Finest Hour

What excuses are likely to keep you away from church? How committed are you to coming every week?

A: There will be a predictable set of answers to this...sleeping in, getting the kids ready on time, using the time to catch up on chores, etc. Look for someone to say something more personal, more revealing, and use that to tactfully challenge others in the group to be more transparent.

Note-taking is just a part of listening skills. How good are you at listening? What strategies can you think of to improve your listening?

A: After a few people have shared their strategies for becoming better listeners, challenge everyone in the group (including yourself) to implement at least one of these ideas.

Session Six : Wrapping It Up

Read Proverbs 28:13. Since God knows all that we do and think anyway, why are we told not to conceal sins from him?

A: To truly repent we must start with admitting that the sin is there in our lives.

NOTES

Other great small-group experiences from Serendipity House...

CANVAS
A DVD-driven small-group experience.

Emerging inside each of us is a unique work of art that reveals who we are and our vital role in the Larger Story. *Canvas* has been created to draw from deep within the stories God has given each of us, and to expose the beauty God is forging from the sum of our experiences. *Canvas* provides the context, the texture, and the materials for the journey. Through your story, your experiences, and the colors of your reality, God works to bring your role in the Larger Story to light.

Distortions Kit 005038463 Experience Guide 005038464
Mystery Kit 005103004 Experience Guide 005103005
Heart Kit 005038428 Experience Guide 005038429

GOD AND THE ARTS
Where faith intersects life.

Stories, great and small, share the same essential structure because every story we tell borrows its power from a Larger Story. What we sense stirring within is a heart that is made for a place in the Larger Story. It is no accident that great movies include a hero, a villain, a betrayal, a battle to fight, a romance, and a beauty to rescue. It is the Epic story and it is truer than anything we know. Adventure awaits. Look closer.

Finding Jesus in the Movies 005038480
Finding Redemption in the Movies 005038469
Finding the Larger Story in Music 005117804

800.458.2772 · www.SerendipityHouse.com